SCIENTIFIC AMERICAN EXPLORES BIG IDEAS

Our Planet, Our Choice

THE SCIENCE OF CLIMATE CHANGE

The Editors of *Scientific American*

SCIENTIFIC AMERICAN EDUCATIONAL PUBLISHING

New York

Published in 2023 by Scientific American Educational Publishing
in association with **The Rosen Publishing Group**
29 East 21st Street, New York, NY 10010

Contains material from Scientific American®, a division of Springer Nature America, Inc., reprinted by permission, as well as original material from The Rosen Publishing Group®.

First Edition

Scientific American
Lisa Pallatroni: Project Editor

Rosen Publishing
Michael Hessel-Mial: Compiling Editor
Michael Moy: Senior Graphic Designer

Cataloging-in-Publication Data
Names: Scientific American, Inc.
Title: Our planet, our choice: the science of climate change / edited by the Editors of Scientific American.
Description: New York : Scientific American Educational Publishing, 2023. | Series: Scientific American explores big ideas | Includes glossary and index.
Identifiers: ISBN 9781684169184 (pbk.) | ISBN 9781684169191 (library bound) | ISBN 9781684169207 (ebook)
Subjects: LCSH: Climatic changes–Juvenile literature. | Climatic changes–Effect of human beings on–Juvenile literature. | Climatic changes–Government policy–Juvenile literature. | Global warming–Juvenile literature. | Global environmental change–Juvenile literature.
Classification: LCC QC903.15 O87 2023 | DDC 363.738'74–dc2

Manufactured in the United States of America
Websites listed were live at the time of publication.

Cover: Sepp photography/Shutterstock.com

CPSIA Compliance Information: Batch #SACS23.
For further information, contact Rosen Publishing at 1-800-237-9932.

CONTENTS

INTRODUCTION

Many books and articles about climate change have emphasized the impacts we'll see far into the future. That is, until we started feeling the effects of climate change in real time. Now, that future isn't an abstraction: climate change is here. The Arctic is melting, droughts and storms are becoming more extreme, and people's daily lives are now subject to climate disruption. *Scientific American* has been a part of the century-long process of understanding climate change in our new, shifting normal.

The articles in this volume are organized in five sections, each focusing on different aspects of modern climate science. The first section summarizes our current understanding of the science and how we know what we know. The second section explores the impact of climate change on the Earth's ecosystems, while the third section focuses specifically on how our society changes with the turbulence of climate change. Articles in the fourth section concern the political debates over climate change, including policy recommendations and the misinformation campaigns that deny climate change is happening. The final section covers some of the proposed technologies to counteract climate change.

Though research on climate change has taken place for decades, this book emphasizes research and writing from the last ten years, to emphasize what themes are most current to the climate crisis, and in science writing more broadly. Science journalism is increasingly informed by the history of science, which is especially important for understanding the phenomenon of climate denial. Likewise, science researchers are more likely to explore the social and political dimensions of scientific questions, because climate change's effects span beyond natural ecology. Lastly, these more current articles reveal that any individual technology alone won't resolve the climate crisis. In debates over specific types of climate responses, we see a need for a broad ranger of perspectives to fully grasp this global problem.

Section 1: Climate Change 101

The Arctic Is Breaking Climate Records, Altering Weather Worldwide

By Jennifer A. Francis

Twenty-five scientists, including me, had an epiphany about the Arctic in 2003. The National Science Foundation had invited us to a retreat in Big Sky, Mont. Before this gathering, each of us had been focusing our Arctic research on our own narrow topics. As we shared our perspectives, we came to a frightening realization: the changes we had been finding individually were connected. They fit together perfectly. The Arctic system as a whole was careening toward a precarious new state. And hope of stopping it already seemed unlikely.

We published a paper with a stunning, controversial conclusion: At the current rate of change, there was a real possibility that within a century, the world could witness a summer Arctic Ocean that would be ice-free, a state not seen for thousands of years. Today I am startled again because it now appears that the ocean will likely be free of summer ice by 2040—a full 60 years earlier than we had predicted more than a decade ago.

The Arctic is changing exactly the way scientists thought it would but faster than even the most aggressive predictions. The recent behavior is off the charts. Since just 2015, more than a dozen climate records that had each stood for many decades have crumbled, including those for disappearing summer sea ice, decreasing winter sea ice, warming air and thawing ground.

These trends signal trouble for people around the world. The last time the Arctic was only slightly warmer than today—about 125,000 years ago—oceans were 13 to 20 feet higher. Goodbye, Miami, New Orleans, the naval base in Norfolk, Va., most of New York City and Silicon Valley, as well as Venice, London and Shanghai. New research suggests that rapid Arctic warming also tends to reroute the jet stream in ways that could allow punishing weather patterns to linger across North America, central Europe and Asia longer than usual, subjecting millions of people to unyielding heat waves, droughts or relentless storms. Plankton are increasing throughout the southern Arctic Ocean, which may disrupt food chains that support commercial fisheries. And the massive ice melt is adding to an enormous blob of freshwater south of Greenland that may be slowing the Gulf Stream, which could significantly change weather patterns for continents on both sides of the Atlantic Ocean.

What's driving this breakneck change?

Loss of "Permanent" Ice

Scientists expend a lot of energy watching the Arctic because it is so sensitive to climatic change. It is a "canary in the coal mine" for the earth's entire climate system. The long list of records that have been smashed during the past several years leaves no doubt that decades of unnerving climate simulations are on target. But the data say something even greater: our projections of changes on the way may be far too conservative.

In only 40 years the extent of ice across the Arctic Ocean in summer has shrunk by half. Yes, half. The volume of sea ice, year-round, is way down, too–about a quarter of what it was in the early 1980s. Until recently, scientists had thought it would take until at least the middle of this century to reach these extremes.

Summer sea ice is vanishing quickly because of feedbacks–vicious cycles that can amplify a small change. For example, when a bit of extra heat melts bright-white ice, more of the dark ocean surface is exposed, which reflects less of the sun's energy back to space. That absorbed heat then warms the area further, which melts even more ice, leading to yet more warming. In winter when the sun is not shining, other feedbacks take over. For example, sea ice floating on the Arctic Ocean acts like an insulating sheet, preventing heat and moisture under it from escaping into the atmosphere. When that ice recedes, more heat and moisture can warm the air, further retarding ice formation. Computer simulations generally show ice disappearing too slowly, contributing to the conservative estimates of future warming.

Disappearing sea ice is not the only transformation keeping researchers like me awake at night. The other two types of what used to be called permanent ice in the Arctic are also declining steeply.

Permafrost–soil that usually remains frozen year-round–has been thawing. Buildings constructed atop permafrost are collapsing, trees are toppling and roads are buckling. In addition to disrupting daily life for local residents, thawing soils also can release large quantities of heat-trapping gases into the atmosphere. When the organic matter that has been locked in permafrost for thousands of years thaws, bacteria break it down into carbon dioxide (if oxygen is present) or methane (if it is not). Arctic permafrost contains about twice as much carbon as the atmosphere holds now, so widespread thaw could greatly exacerbate global warming–which would lead to even faster thaw. Today's computer models do not adequately capture the impacts of thawing permafrost, again contributing to substantial underestimates of future global warming.

The third type of previously permanent Arctic ice is the frozen water on land, including glaciers and Greenland's enormous ice cap, which is more than a mile thick on average. Losing this ice has dire consequences worldwide because, unlike melting sea ice, the runoff into the ocean raises sea level directly. During the summer of 2016 the total mass of Greenland's ice sheet (estimated using satellite measurements of how it affects the earth's gravity) reached the smallest value since satellite observations began in 2002. The levels are also lower than any amount going back to the late 1950s, when the mass was estimated in other ways. A recent investigation suggests that the accelerating ice melt on Greenland's surface is hastened by warming effects linked to dwindling sea ice.

Hotter, Wetter Air

Reduced sea ice and rapid Arctic warming have other far-reaching effects. The combination may alter upper-level winds so that they carry additional heat and moisture from southerly latitudes toward the North Pole. In 2012 the then record Greenland surface melt resulted from an unusually strong and persistent ridge of high pressure in the atmosphere—a so-called blocking high. It brought not only heat and moisture from the south but also soot from wildfires around the Northern Hemisphere. That soot darkens ice and snow surfaces (lowering its albedo, or reflectivity), which then absorb more of the sun's energy, accelerating melt—another one of those vicious cycles.

Blocking patterns—large eddies in the jet stream—near Greenland appear to be occurring more often in recent decades, especially in summer months, which probably accounts for at least part of the upward trend in melting. Ice-mass loss during 2018–2019 set a new record, topping 2010 and 2012. Recent work by my colleagues and me suggests that the greater number of blocking highs most likely is tied to global warming. Computer simulations struggle to form and break down blocks realistically, however, so it is hard to say how these patterns may act in the future.

Other Arctic behavior is equally outlandish. During the winters since 2016, record-breaking heat waves near the North Pole were surpassed by more record-breaking heat waves. Waning and thinning sea ice is part of the cause, providing less of a barrier for the ocean's heat to enter the air. The jet stream's wild north-south swings also brought record pulses of warmth and moisture to far northern latitudes. Scientists and Arctic residents often fail to appreciate the strong effects that the extra moisture can create. For starters, water vapor is a greenhouse gas, so in a dry Arctic winter atmosphere, a little more moisture can trap substantially more heat. Moreover, when that moisture condenses into clouds, it releases latent heat, further warming the air. Finally, more clouds trap more warmth below them, one more factor contributing to the Arctic meltdown.

Stuck in Extremes

Although we have more to learn, it has become clear that rapid Arctic change is underway, the most dramatic in human history.

Given this stark reality, atmospheric scientists are trying to pin down the effects that the changing Arctic may have on people and ecosystems around the world so society can decide how to react and prepare for the future.

An obvious example of global effects is coastal flooding. According to a 2017 report by the Union of Concerned Scientists, about 170 U.S. coastal communities will experience chronic inundation within 20 years. By the end of this century, if nations keep emitting carbon dioxide as they have been, most large coastal cities around the world will face regular, disruptive flooding. This eerily prescient report was published just weeks before Hurricanes Harvey, Irma and Maria capped the U.S.'s most destructive and costly hurricane season ever.

There is also mounting evidence that strong warm-ups in the Arctic's lower atmosphere can affect winds in the jet stream and even higher, in the stratosphere, home to the polar vortex wind pattern that circles the Arctic. Northward peaks and southward valleys in the bending jet stream generate the high- and low-pressure centers we see on weather maps as a capital H or L. The bends control our weather in the Northern Hemisphere. But if extremely large bends occur more often, we can expect to see an uptick in extreme conditions where billions of people live. That is because large bends in the jet stream tend to progress more slowly from west to east, causing the weather systems they create to hang around longer. Think prolonged heat waves, relentless rains and stalled tropical storms like Hurricane Harvey, which swamped Houston in August 2017—as well as more intense fire seasons like the ones California has experienced in recent years.

Large waves in the jet stream, along with strong Arctic warming, can disrupt the polar vortex, prolonging deadly deep freezes or parades of snowstorms, including the devastating stretch of severe cold that gripped the lower Midwest U.S. in February 2021. A polar vortex collapse can also perpetuate wild jet-stream swings that deliver intense heat waves to Alaska and the far north, creating yet another vicious cycle that accelerates Arctic warming. Some studies suggest that Arctic warming is closely connected with these wavy patterns; others say proof of the connection is still tenuous. Research on this hot topic is advancing quickly.

A rapidly warming Arctic most likely will significantly alter habitats on land and at sea. Already, as sea ice recedes, plankton blooms have appeared in new areas during new seasons, enticing species of fish from lower latitudes to move into Arctic waters while native fish disappear. Earlier spring snowmelt across high latitudes has led to earlier greening of the tundra and earlier hatching of insects; migrating birds, which take their cues from the length of daylight hours, may arrive at Arctic food sites too late for the feast. Peoples of the Arctic are feeling the impacts, too; melting ice is keeping them from traditional hunting grounds and even forcing them to uproot towns threatened by coastal erosion from high storm waves in areas that used to be protected by ice along the shore. At the same time, big countries and big companies are swooping in to search for newly accessible natural resources, as tensions rise over who can claim which parts of the vast, rich seabed as theirs.

The revelation my colleagues and I had at the Big Sky retreat replays in my head every time another long-lived weather pattern wreaks havoc or another Arctic record is broken. Now my neighbors are catching on. Polls suggest that most Americans think that the loss of Arctic ice and the jet stream—which has fast become a household term—are conspiring to create weird weather. The old Arctic may have been ruthless, but it was stable. The new Arctic is less predictable and may be changing in ways that are irreversible, with ripple effects on life around the globe.

Are these impacts still avoidable? Yes and no. Because the climate's response lags behind the increases in greenhouse gas concentrations and because carbon dioxide has a very long lifetime in the atmosphere, future change is already baked into the system. But the magnitude and pace can be reduced if society moves quickly to drastically cut emissions and if methods can be developed to extract carbon from the atmosphere in large quantities. Progress on both these fronts is rapid, though likely too little, too late, to preserve the earth and the Arctic as we have known them. Prepare for the unexpected.

Referenced

Arctic Matters: The Global Connection to Changes in the Arctic. National Research Council. National Academies Press, 2015.

Amplified Arctic Warming and Mid-latitude Weather: New Perspectives on Emerging Connections. Jennifer A. Francis, Stephen J. Vavrus and Judah Cohen in *WIREs Climate Change*, Vol. 8, No. 5, Article. No. e474; September/October 2017.

About the Author

Jennifer A. Francis is a senior scientist and acting deputy director of the Woodwell Climate Research Center. She has done extensive research on Arctic warming and on atmospheric vapor and energy. She is a member of Scientific American's board of advisers.

What Ancient Mass Extinctions Tell Us about the Future

By Peter Brannen

Pangaea, 252 million years ago—the world is over. Siberia has been erupting for 300,000 years, is still erupting and won't stop. Not a volcano, mind you, but Siberia—two million square miles of it. A suppurating, billowing, continent-scaled wasteland of glowing rock and steam. The seas, once resplendent with horn corals and sponge reefs, are now sour and laden with mercury. Hot as soup, they bubble deathly swamp gas that feeds vile, hurricane-churned slicks of slime. The seabed is vacant, as scuttling trilobites die out after a quarter of a billion years. Beside this rancid ocean, on the shores of a blasted supercontinent, the forests are gone. Instead hot rivers now spill over the dead land in wide braids. Fungus blooms where vanished groves of ferns once held contests full of fangs and armor—gorgonopsids battling pareiasaurs. Their final bones are now scoured by hot winds and bleached by a searing sunlight, unfiltered by ozone. Night falls and brings odd constellations that light the dead waves, lapping at dead shores, tossing old bits of a dead reef from a dead sea. It smells awful. The planet is ruin and slime and heat. The ocean suffocates. Bacterial mounds spread. A hundred thousand suns rise and fall on a hopeless world. A hundred thousand springtimes arrive with no respite. It's still all but barren. A million years of misery pass. Ten million.

At long last, the planet is finally reborn—this time with dinosaurs and ichthyosaurs and pterosaurs and mammals and turtles and sturgeon—almost as if a new story entirely has begun, exuberant, confident, vital: the Mesozoic era. The old story, too dark to retell, has long been filed away somewhere deep in the great cabinets of Earth, along with an epitaph in the rocks, written in geochemistry: carbon dioxide destroyed this world.

Mass extinctions are not merely bad days in Earth history. They are not even very bad days. They are the very, very worst days in the entire half-billion-year history of complex life. They are supremely horrifying, astronomically rare, global Ragnaroks that end the lineages of most living creatures on the planet. They are terrible, surreal things: 20,000 years of suffocating greenhouse heat punctuated by volcanic winter blasts or an afternoon of celestial terror and tsunamis. And until around 1980, they were mostly thought to be disreputable speculation.

Over the past two centuries the field of geology, like the fossil record itself, has been characterized by long periods of stasis punctuated by exhilarating moments of upheaval and innovation. It would be arbitrary to identify *one* founding figure for the modern study of geology, but one could do worse than Scottish geologist James Hutton, who did much to reveal the "abyss of time" underneath us. At a salt-sprayed Siccar Point on the eastern coast of Scotland in 1788, he spied an outcrop made of two kinds of rock, one stacked on top of the other, meeting abruptly in the middle. But the rock on the bottom—laminations of deep-sea muck—had been formed at the bottom of the ocean, tilted sideways, thrust up into the air and planed off by wind and erosion. And the rock on the top had been formed by tropical rivers on dry land. The missing time implied between the two rocks, now conjoined but separated by an unthinkable gap, shattered Hutton. The body of his writing is notoriously obtuse and unimpressive; he apparently saved all his eloquence for one haunting observation that, in the confusion of Earth beneath our feet, "we find no vestige of a beginning, no prospect of an end." Although the history of humanity has played out in the shallows so far, time, it turns out, is *deep*.

Geologists cast off the strictures of biblical time and Noah's flood, and their new field matured over the decades, spurred by a significant material reward for finding coal and minerals in a strange new industrial age. The story of life on Earth, however fragmentary and tantalizing, slowly revealed itself.

At this magazine's founding in the mid-1800s, the field was in its adolescence. It was still dominated by men of means—the kind of ascotted dilettantes rendered humorlessly in oil and lithograph portraits. The contributions of women such as Mary Anning, the unmatched fossil hunter who scoured the English shoreline unearthing the local "snakestones" and "stone crocodiles" that littered the wave-battered Jurassic Coast, were acknowledged only sheepishly. Although *Scientific American* headlines from the time still hint at a somewhat rudimentary state of affairs ("Experts Doubt the Sun Is Actually Burning Coal"), by midcentury geology had nonetheless been established as an empirical, systematized field of inquiry with roots in antiquity—one of the many such intellectual eddies that swirled out of Enlightenment-era "natural philosophy." That is, it now had rules. The rules were deceptively simple and powerful. Layers of ocean rock now propped up at unusual angles on land must have once laid flat on a seafloor in some distant age. Dikes of old magma that pierced this stony tiramisu must have worked their shoots into the layered rock sometime after. The fossils entombed in these rock layers could be correlated to those fossils and those rocks with the same layers, way over there.

In 1860 English geologist John Phillips drew on the fossil-collecting labor of decades prior, and a growing body of paleontology literature scattered across elegant monographs, to plot a surprisingly modern curve of the richness of life over Earth history, the first ever such diagram. The graph ominously included two profound dips in life: one crash that separated the trilobite-spangled Paleozoic era from the dinosaur-haunted Mesozoic era and another plunge that separated the Mesozoic from our own Cenozoic time (all terms of Phillips's invention). The dramatic breaks in fossil life hinted at some kind of ancient calamity that divided the great ages and supported the blasphemous idea that species—that is, God's very Creation—might go extinct, which had been proposed half a century earlier by the renowned French naturalist Georges Cuvier. On considering the odd elephant bones that littered the New World, of mammoths and mastodons ("*animal de l'Ohio*"), Cuvier had proposed that life on Earth, like French rule, could be swept away in "revolutions." Phillips's graph provided something close to quantitative proof, and Phillips himself thought that each recovery consisted of separate acts of divine creation. Yet it would take more than a century for anyone to take the idea of mass extinctions seriously again.

This is because, by the end of the 19th century, the field was still dominated, and would continue to be dominated for decades, by the enduring framework of "uniformitarianism." This concept, popularized by Charles Lyell, is summarized in a catchphrase still taught to geology students: "The present is the key to the past." That is, the unhurried processes at work on the face of Earth today–the relentless if unimpressive work of rain on rock, the inexorable incision of rivers into highlands or the piling of sand into desert dunes–have always been plying the planet in the same tedious fashion and could account for everything we find in the rock record. Painting on this vast new canvas of time, Charles Darwin would propose that similarly small but steady biological changes over generations, filtered by the relentless tournament of life and death, and given Hutton's eons to ramify, could produce the "endless forms" of life "most beautiful" on Earth today. Pointedly absent from this measured account of planetary history were the gauche cataclysms of Cuvier and Phillips.

Geology was upended in the middle of the 20th century by the plate tectonic revolution–the validation of the once fringe idea that continents drifted across the world like rudderless ships. Even so, the idea of sudden apocalyptic global mass extinctions remained suspect at best. Catastrophism was spooky, reminiscent of a benighted prescientific world where capricious gods subjected the world to cleansing acts of global destruction. Worse, speculation about why the dinosaurs had disappeared had become something of a cottage industry among cranks, and serious scientists were nervous about associating with a crowd who proposed, among dozens of other incoherent ideas for their demise, "dwindling brain and consequent stupidity," development of heads that became "too heavy to lift," "psychotic suicidal factors," "competition with caterpillars," "terminal hay fever" and "methane poisoning from dinosaur flatulence." And yet the orthodoxy began to crack.

"*Neokatastrophismus?*" the iconoclastic German scientist Otto Schindewolf asked of his fellow paleontologists in 1963, attempting to revive Cuvier's catastrophism for the 20th century. Because his question was posed in German, few English-speaking scientists felt the need to reply. But Schindewolf could no longer overlook the ominous interruption of life he saw—among other places—exposed in the ancient rocks of the Salt Range in Pakistan. There appeared to be a dreadful global collapse of the ocean ecosystem at the end of the Permian period a quarter of a billion years ago (in fact, the greatest mass extinction in Earth history), just as Phillips had plotted more than a century prior. Schindewolf conscripted a supernova for his vision of the apocalypse, proposing that it might have irradiated Earth and seeded the biosphere with ruinous mutations.

In that same year American Norman Newell, plotting the fates of 2,500 animal families over Earth history, noted six intervals when extinction seemed to cut a broad swath through all of life, instead proposing dramatic sea-level changes as his preferred Grim Reaper. And at the end of the decade Digby McLaren, director of the Canadian Geological Survey's Institute of Sedimentary and Petroleum Geology, insisted in his 1969 presidential address to the Paleontological Society that his fellow paleontologists were trying to "define out of existence" the obvious breaks in the fossil record, such as a devastating wave of death 375 million years ago that wiped out the largest global reef system in the history of life. "I cannot accept a uniformitarian explanation," he said of the catastrophe, glaringly apparent in ancient rocks from Iran to Alberta. McLaren had an idea for what could cause such a discontinuity.

"I shall, therefore, land a large or very large meteorite in the Paleozoic Pacific," he announced, capable of generating "a wave twenty thousand feet high. This will do." McLaren's address, it is reported, was "met with embarrassed silence," and many paleontologists in the audience, still under Lyell's spell, assumed he must have been joking.

Then, in 1980, an asteroid landed in the field. Walter Alvarez, then a young University of California, Berkeley, professor, was traipsing the Apennines above the medieval Italian town of Gubbio. In this mountainous pile of ancient limestone seafloor, pushed up by the grinding advance of Africa into Europe, there was a sharp break—a lifeless clay layer—between the placid sea life of dinosaur times and the impoverished life of the early age of mammals. Perhaps this transformative interval took place over millions of years, validating the uniformitarian view. Or perhaps Cuvier and Phillips had it right all along, and the turnover was devastatingly short. Curious, Alvarez recruited his father, Luis, a Nobel-winning physicist, to help tackle the question. It was quite the second act for the elder Alvarez, a pioneer of military radar technology and Manhattan Project alum who helped to develop the atomic bomb and even watched "Little Boy" explode over Hiroshima from an attending B-29. His wartime work became unexpectedly relevant to the catastrophe they were investigating, which throttled the planet some 66 million years earlier.

The Alvarezes knew that unusual elements like iridium were delivered to Earth from above by an eternal drizzle of space dust, at a steady rate. Measure the iridium in the ominous clay layer, they reasoned, and if there's just a little bit, the dramatic turnover in life couldn't have taken very long. Conversely, if there's a lot of iridium, it took a very long time indeed. But what if, as they discovered, there was 100 times more iridium than they ever expected? After bombarding the clay samples with neutrons from a nuclear reactor and analyzing them, the Alvarezes were astonished. The only vehicle large enough for this much exotic material was not a light drizzle of space dust but one truly gigantic space rock. (Often omitted in this account, though not by the Alvarezes themselves, is the fact that Dutch geologist Jan Smit and Belgian geologist Jan Hertogen made the very same discovery among ancient ocean rocks in Spain at the very same time and even published their results in the journal *Nature* two weeks earlier than the Alvarezes' landmark *Science* paper.)

The resulting chaos from such an impact would be like all-out nuclear warfare, only worse. There would be the unimaginable heat from the initial explosion, which would have been thousands of times more powerful than the detonation of all the nuclear weapons on Earth at the height of the cold war, all in one place, all at once. "Certainly enough," as one impact modeler put it to me, "to lift a mountain back into space at escape velocity." It has been proposed that as this spacebound ejecta encircled the globe, it might have turned the atmosphere into a pizza oven for 20 minutes (with dinosaurs playing the role of pepperoni). Then there might have been the decades of darkness and cold from the nuclear winter to follow, starving any lingering creature lucky enough to have avoided being evaporated outright by the asteroid, swept up in its tsunamis, or turned to charcoal by the ballistic reentry of its debris into the atmosphere.

In 1991 whatever lingering skepticism about the impact that remained among uniformitarian hardliners was wiped away by the discovery of a 110-mile crater buried under tens of millions of years of limestone on Mexico's Yucatán peninsula. In fact, the crater had already been discovered in 1978 by geophysicists working for the Mexican national oil company Pemex, but they had announced their findings at a geophysics conference that had escaped notice of paleontologists for more than a decade. And the structure had been found some 1,000 years earlier by the Maya, who built settlements around limestone sinkholes that pock the Yucatán and that provided freshwater. The pattern of these sinkholes reflects the deeply disturbed rock far below and maps almost exactly onto the crater's edge, in a 110-mile ring.

Popular culture took note. The 1990s saw a rash of impact-inspired cable specials and movies strewn with bad CGI, which—along with the astounding, apocalypse-scaled collision of Comet Shoemaker-Levy 9 with Jupiter in 1994—were sufficient to convince the public of the dangers of space rocks. This is typically where the story ends. As far as most people are concerned, mass extinctions are what happen when big things fall out of the sky.

But something funny happened over the next 30 years as geologists fanned out across the globe to look for convincing evidence of impacts—such as layers of iridium, shocked quartz or giant craters—at the ominous rock boundaries that mark the four other major mass extinctions in Earth history. They didn't find any. And all but one of the so-called Big Five mass extinctions were *even more severe* than the catastrophe that wiped out the nonbird dinosaurs.

In fact, there even existed major impact structures, such as the Triassic-age 62-mile-wide Manicouagan Crater in Quebec (now a circular system of lakes amid a boreal paradise of blackflies) or the massive crater that created the Chesapeake Bay 36 million years ago, that did not seem to bother life much at all. Given the remarkable correlation of the Yucatán impact with the disappearance of the large dinosaurs (and much of the rest of life on Earth at the end of the Cretaceous period), this came as a surprise. Stranger still, the stunning finale of the age of dinosaurs was also accompanied not only by an envoy from outer space but by one of the largest volcanic events in the history of animal life: a swath of eruptions that drowned much of India *miles* deep in lava. While the consensus is that the asteroid did most of the damage, this was the same class of world-changing eruptions responsible not only for dozens of minor mass extinctions and climate misadventures throughout Earth history but several of the other major mass extinctions as well, including the worst ever at the end of the Permian 252 million years ago.

In the past few decades a subtler story about mass extinctions has emerged. Geologists are now armed with powerful techniques Hutton couldn't have dreamed of. Scattering to remote rock outcrops around the world or to archives of muck hoisted from the bottom of the ocean by drill ships, they wring secrets out of old seashells with mass spectrometers, and from age-battered hunks of granite with radioisotope geochronology, and from fossil and geochemical databases with neural networks underwritten by blistering processing power. And in this diffuse project to understand Earth history, geologists have in recent years revealed a roster of existential threats to life far more intimate than simply death from above. The most frequent mass killer of life on Earth, it turns out, is Earth itself. And the most reliable murder weapon is carbon dioxide.

One hundred and thirty-five million years before a mindless hunk of space garbage intercepted Earth's orbit and ruined a perfectly good dinosaur world, the planet was gripped by a mass extinction that was even worse. A world of bizarre crocodilians, giant amphibians, stony corals, a ubiquity of strange but venerable eel-like creatures, and 80 percent of the rest of complex life on Earth was destroyed. As the supercontinent Pangaea pulled apart at the seams, stretching like taffy, an open sore of oozing, incandescent rock erupted at the surface, covering three million square miles in lava in pulses over 600,000 years. While the eruptions would have caused all sorts of chaos, perhaps most important they injected thousands of gigatons of carbon dioxide into the atmosphere, and the oceans overdosed on this volcanic CO2. The seawater acidified as a simple matter of chemistry, and the temperature of the planet soared as a simple matter of physics. This is what CO2 does. Today the New Jersey Palisades across the Hudson River from New York City are the volcanic plumbing that remains from these titanic eruptions of the Triassic end times, old magma that is matched by the same volcanic rock, of the same age, as far afield as Morocco, Brazil, Nova Scotia and Spain.

Hundreds of millions of years earlier the two oldest major mass extinctions destroyed planets we wouldn't recognize, their continents misshapen and scattered about unfamiliar oceans. The oceans of these alien planets were patrolled by gigantic cephalopods and, later, even more gigantic fish, guillotine-mawed and fortified by helmets of bone. Our planet endlessly cycles carbon—the stuff of life—through rocks, air, water and life in a balance that keeps the climate habitable and ocean chemistry hospitable. But these archaic worlds saw this carbon cycle suddenly derailed—unraveled by CO2-sucking episodes of tropical mountain building, accelerated rock weathering and the novel global geoengineering project of land plants. These kill mechanisms are somewhat more convoluted, and admittedly less dramatic, than an asteroid, but they did the trick. These bygone planets spun out of control, alternately freezing and broiling as Earth struggled to regain its composure and wrangle a global carbon cycle gone haywire.

But it was 252 million years ago, on the forsaken planet that opened this tour of ancient apocalypses—that sun-bleached world, with oceans almost absent of animals—when the story of life on Earth nearly came to its premature conclusion. This was Pangaea, a world before dinosaurs or mammals or flowers. But it was still a rich world, one with conifers and lithe, vaguely leonine predators and lumbering, warty, reptile prey. And then, it was over. It ended in a continent-scaled flood of glowing rock, brief volcanic winters issuing from the eruptions and a roster of billowing volcanic gases, many of which would be banned on a battlefield—such as chlorine gas and mercury.

As the magma incinerated underground seams of salt and gypsum, eruptions of halocarbons would have obliterated the ozone layer—and indeed, plant fossils bear the mutations wrought by this ancient atmospheric destruction. But it wasn't until the seams of magma feeding these eruptions hit huge deposits of natural gas, coal and carbon-rich rocks underground that the greatest mass extinction ever hit its appalling crescendo. Methane and carbon dioxide exploded out of the ground by the tens of thousands of gigatons. Temperatures spiked by almost 22 degrees Fahrenheit. And in the oceans, where spreading anoxia and acidification wiped out 96 percent of life, it was as hot as a jacuzzi. And then, in the fossil record, silence.

At the start of the industrial revolution, long slumbering forests of carbon were resurrected from the ancient Earth and pressed into service in the furnaces of modernity. We know that this artificial fire can't go on forever without immiserating our world. At 416 parts per million, carbon dioxide is already higher than it has been in millions of years and is perhaps rising even faster than in these greatest calamities of all time. Meanwhile centuries—millennia even—of hunting, land clearing and pollution have impoverished the natural world. By one estimate, at the rate at which we are currently driving species extinct, we could match the biological devastation of those towering mass extinctions of the ancient past within 300 to 12,000 years. This might sound like a long time frame, but from a geologic perspective, it is downright subliminal. More worryingly, there may yet exist unseen ecological cliff edges along the way, beyond which the biosphere does not simply suffer the onslaught of attrition but collapses suddenly in cascading failures. In other words, there may be tipping points—points of no return.

We know what we have to do to avoid being inducted into the wretched Pantheon of the worst things that have ever happened in Earth history. We must set aside swaths of the planet—in the form of marine protected areas, natural reserves and corridors for migration—to allow the living world to recover from the uppercut we have already delivered it. Then, we must simply stop digging up old life from deep in Earth's crust and lighting it on fire at the surface. As humanity leans on the very same levers pulled in the very worst things that have ever happened in history, we must consult the ages and listen to the counsel of broken worlds past.

About the Author

Peter Brannen is a science journalist whose book The Ends of the World *is about the five major mass extinctions (Ecco, 2017). Brannen was a 2018–2019 Scripps Fellow at the University of Colorado Boulder.*

The Hidden Figure in Climate Science

By Dawn Starin

John Tyndall was a mountaineer, prolific writer of science books, prominent physicist and professor of natural philosophy at the Royal Institution of Great Britain. He was also an original member of the X Club, an exclusive scientific dining club whose members were frequent contributors to the well-regarded journal *Nature*.

With his doctorate, easy access to the Royal Institution's laboratories, and social and intellectual friendships and networks with some of the greatest minds of the Victorian period, it is not surprising that Tyndall reached the heights of scientific achievement and recognition.

For more than 160 years Irish-born Tyndall has been credited with the original discovery of the absorption of thermal radiation by carbon dioxide and water vapor–the very cornerstone of our current understanding of climate change, weather and meteorology. He was the first to clearly demonstrate and understand the physical basis of the greenhouse effect.

Another first originated with a hidden figure in the history of climate science, one who remained unacknowledged until brought to light in 2011 by independent researcher Raymond Sorenson. Later researched by writer John Perlin and the main subject of a symposium held in May 2018 at the University of California, Santa Barbara, this previously unknown contributor to our current understanding of climate change was an American amateur scientist, a suffragette and a woman: Eunice Newton Foote, born 200 years ago.

Three years before Tyndall first published his broad findings in the *Proceedings of the Royal Society of London* in 1859, Foote demonstrated the absorption of solar heat by carbon dioxide and water vapor and wrote up her findings in a paper entitled "Circumstances Affecting the Heat of the Sun's Rays." While Foote did not differentiate between heat from the whole solar spectrum and long-wave infrared, which is actually responsible for the greenhouse effect, she does seem to be the first to suggest that changing amounts of carbon dioxide and water vapor could alter the climate. Tyndall understood the difference, though he did not use the term "long-wave infrared" because it was not yet invented.

Certainly, Tyndall's equipment, laboratory and experimental results were more sophisticated than Foote's, and he is rightly credited with establishing the experimental basis for the greenhouse effect, first suggested by Swiss physicist Horace Bénédict de Saussure in the the 1760s and later developed by French mathematician Joseph Fourier in the 1820s and French physicist Claude Pouillet in 1836. And yet, while acknowledging these men's work, Tyndall did not reference Foote's. Why?

There is some debate about whether Tyndall even knew of Foote's work, though there was some mention of her paper in various North American publications. For example, the September 13, 1856, issue of *Scientific American*, reported that her experiment on the effects of the sun's rays on different gases afforded "abundant evidence of the ability of woman to investigate any subject with originality and precision."

According to Roland Jackson, Tyndall's biographer, general editor of his correspondence and past chief executive of the British Science Association, it seems safe to assume that "if anyone had seen it and understood its significance, there would be some evidence of this, as they would have informed Tyndall and/or each other." But to date, not a single reference to her work has been found in any letter, journal or publication of the major contemporary figures in this field. Therefore, it seems most likely that very little, if any, significant discussion or proper citations or summaries of her study reached England during the time Tyndall was working on and publishing his research.

Did Tyndall know about Foote's work and simply ignore it because she was an amateur, an American or a woman? Perhaps. During Victorian England, a prejudice against amateurs, Americans and women as not quite as capable or professional as British men existed. And Tyndall was no democrat and no supporter of female emancipation.

Did he know about the significance of Foote's study and actively plagiarized it? Maybe, although, as Jackson points out, this would be entirely out of character and extremely risky. Furthermore, both Jackson and Ed Hawkins, a climate scientist at the National Center for Atmospheric Science and the University of Reading in England, feel that if Tyndall had actually known about Foote's results, he would have started his experiments using CO2 and water vapor. He didn't: Tyndall initially tried dry air, oxygen, hydrogen and nitrogen before experimenting on CO2 and water vapor.

Is the lack of credit for Foote linked to insufficient information, prejudice or a deliberate omission on Tyndall's part? Whatever the truth is, and we may never know, it is now clear that Foote's experiment added to the understanding of climate science. As Katharine Hayhoe, co-director of the Climate Science Center at Texas Tech University, has pointed out, while Foote's research did not directly establish the physical basis of what we now call the greenhouse effect, she appears to have been the first person to notice the ability of carbon dioxide and water vapor to absorb heat and to make a direct link between the variability of these atmospheric constituents and climate change.

For this achievement, Foote clearly deserves a place on the pantheon of past and present climate scientists and those to come in the future.

This was originally published as an opinion piece. The views expressed are those of the author(s) and are not necessarily those of Scientific American.

About the Author

Dawn Starin, an anthropologist, has spent decades doing research, mostly in Africa and Asia. Her articles have appeared in publications as varied as Behaviour, Critical Asian Studies, The Ecologist, Gastronomica, The Humanist, Journal of the Royal Society of Medicine, The New York Times, and Philosophy Now.

Global Warming: How Hot, Exactly, Is It Going to Get?

By Kate Marvel

Imagine spending your whole career working on a question to which you don't want to know the answer. We know that greenhouse gas emissions can and do warm the planet, but we don't know one very basic thing: How hot, exactly, is it going to get? The main reason for this, of course, is that human behavior is so hard to predict. How will the people of the late 21st century get their energy? Will they need as much as we do, or will they have fundamentally different lives?

Perhaps that decision will have been made for them by war or societal collapse. None of this is knowable. But even if we could remove all the uncertainty associated with politics, economics, technology and demography, we still wouldn't be sure. There are many things we don't understand about our rapidly warming planet.

To some extent, we know why we don't know. I have been sternly informed by communications experts that "global warming" is a better term for what's happening than "climate change." I have also been told the opposite. Yet the two are inseparable: they feed back on each other. Rising temperatures change the planet, and these changes can speed up or, if we are very lucky, slow down the warming we've caused.

We are not very lucky. Most of these changes will make things worse. The polar ice that we are currently melting is a good example. Right now it reflects sunlight back to space, cooling the planet like a sunscreen on a car windshield. When it goes, it will leave behind dark land or ocean to absorb rather than reflect the sun. A little bit of warming can become much more.

To study the effects of these changes, we use something artificial but useful: the concept of climate "sensitivity." In our climate models, we abruptly double atmospheric carbon dioxide from its preindustrial value of 280 parts per million, let the model Earth evolve for a few hundred years and then measure the increase in its temperature. In the first generation of climate models, this varied from about 1.5 degrees Celsius to about 4.5. The best guess was about three degrees C. The next time we did this, having improved the models substantially, the best guess was three degrees, and the range was between 1.5 and 4.5 degrees. After decades of new science and advances in computing power later, nothing about these estimates or their uncertainty has substantially changed.

We don't know everything, but we know more than nothing. All climate models simulate a changing planet in response to a changing temperature. And increasingly, we know why they disagree on that final warming. In the climate models that warm, more low, thick clouds appear to be changing in ways that reduce their sun-blocking power. In the models that warm less, these changes are smaller.

So scientists have devoted their time to measuring clouds, understanding them and figuring out how to represent them in climate models. This work has paid off: the range of uncertainty is now changing. Unfortunately, it has increased. Climate models that use more modern techniques to simulate clouds are now projecting more warming: five or six degrees C in response to a doubling of carbon dioxide. To put those numbers in context, 4.5 degrees is the difference between now and the last ice age.

I find these high numbers hard to believe, but as a scientist it's my job to find things hard to believe. My skepticism is rooted in clues from the planet's past. At the height of the last ice age, temperatures were cooler and carbon dioxide levels lower. It's hard to reconcile these measurements with extremely high climate sensitivities. But it's almost impossible to reconcile them with extremely low ones.

Clues from the more recent past might seem to paint a more reassuring picture. We have, after all, emitted carbon dioxide, and the planet has warmed in response. Earth is about one degree C warmer than it was before the Industrial Revolution. This is dangerous but not yet catastrophic, and some have suggested that it might be indicative of a planet relatively insensitive to carbon dioxide. But the past is not the future, and we have good reason to believe that there are no analogues for the future into which we are hurtling. Right now heat is being mixed into the deep ocean, which is cold and vast but not infinite. It will warm up in time, over hundreds or thousands of years, and the changes it will trigger may be different than any we have ever observed. Clouds may dissipate, ice will melt and the warming will get worse.

These uncertainties matter in the real world. If the climate is very sensitive to carbon dioxide–if the changes provoked by warming themselves create much more warming–then our time frame for action is reduced. If the climate is relatively insensitive, then perhaps we'll have a little more breathing room. But we have ruled out a climate sensitivity of zero. Warming is real, it's happening and it's likely to get worse. Uncertainty is no excuse for inaction. Even in the improbable event that climate sensitivity is very low, "business as usual" still warms the planet and leads to unpleasant consequences. In the event that climate sensitivity is high, "business as usual" means disaster.

Climate models, like all models, are imperfect representations of the real world. They tell us something useful about the planet we are changing but not how much, exactly, we'll change it. The only way to be sure is to actually double atmospheric carbon dioxide and wait until the planet approaches a new equilibrium, measuring the changes along the way. This is an uncontrolled experiment I hope will never come to pass. But I'm afraid we're well on our way to finding out what will happen if it does.

About the Author

Kate Marvel is a climate scientist at Columbia University and NASA's Goddard Institute for Space Studies. She received a Ph.D. in theoretical physics from the University of Cambridge and has worked at Stanford University, the Carnegie Institution and Lawrence Livermore National Laboratory. Her writing has appeared in Scientific American, *the* On Being *podcast and* Nautilus *magazine. Marvel has given talks in places as diverse as comedy clubs, prisons and the* TED *main stage.*

Why We Know about the Greenhouse Gas Effect

By David Wogan

Our understanding of how certain atmospheric gases trap heat dates back almost 200 years to 1824 when Joseph Fourier described what we know as the greenhouse effect. Fourier, a French mathematician and physicist, asked what seems to be a simple question: why doesn't the planet keep heating up as it receives sunlight? What is regulating our atmospheric temperature?

Knowing that heated surfaces emit radiation (thermal energy), Fourier reasoned that the Earth would emit radiation absorbed by the Sun back into space – resulting in an icy planet. There must be something regulating the temperature – emitting enough thermal energy to keep the planet from freezing and overheating. Not too hot, not too cold.

Fourier's answer to these questions is formalized in what we now call the greenhouse gas effect. From the American Institute of Physics history of climate change page:

> How does the Earth's blanket of air impede the outgoing heat radiation? Fourier tried to explain his insight by comparing the Earth with its covering of air to a box with a glass cover. That was a well-known experiment – the box's interior warms up when sunlight enters while the heat cannot escape. This was an over simple explanation, for it is quite different physics that keeps heat inside an actual glass box, or similarly in a greenhouse. (As Fourier knew, the main effect of the glass is to keep the air, heated by contact with sun-warmed surfaces, from wafting away. The glass does also keep heat radiation from escaping, but that's less important.) Nevertheless, people took up his analogy and trapping of heat by the atmosphere eventually came to be called "the greenhouse effect."

Fourier's work was instrumental in understanding climate change. Years after Fourier's death on May 16, 1830, scientists continued to ask questions about the greenhouse gas effect. In 1862, John Tyndall discovered that certain gases (water and carbon dioxide) help trap heat from escaping the atmosphere. Later, in 1895, Swedish Chemist Svante Arrhenius observed the infrared-absorbing properties of carbon dioxide and water molecules.

We still see the impact of Fourier's answer today, with the recent news that atmospheric carbon dioxide measurements surpassed 400 parts per million, and the ongoing debates of how to limit and adapt to a changing climate. It is, you might say, a hot topic.

This was originally published as an opinion piece. The views expressed are those of the author(s) and are not necessarily those of Scientific American.

About the Author

David Wogan is an engineer and policy researcher who writes about energy, technology, and policy. David's academic and professional background includes a unique blend of technology and policy in the field of energy systems. Most recently, David worked at Austin Energy, a Texas municipal utility, implementing a Department of Energy stimulus grant related to energy efficiency. Previously, David was a member of the Energy & Climate Change team at the White House Council on Environmental Quality for the Obama Administration. David holds two Master's degrees from The University of Texas at Austin in Mechanical Engineering and Public Affairs. While at UT, David was a researcher in the Webber Energy Group, where his research focused on advanced biofuel production to offset petroleum use in the transportation sector. David holds a Bachelor's of Science degree in Mechanical Engineering from The University of Texas at Austin, where he researched nuclear non-proliferation measurement technology. David is a 2013 Aspen Institute Journalism Scholar, joining a select group of journalists from Slate, ABC News, and The New York Times.

Section 2: Ecological Impacts of Climate Change

Marine Oxygen Levels Are the Next Great Casualty of Climate Change

By Nathalie Goodkin, Julie Pullen

Last summer, in an unseasonal event, more than 100 miles of Florida's coast around Tampa Bay became an oxygen-depleted dead zone littered with fish along the nearby shoreline. In the Northwest, Dungeness crabs were washing onto Oregon's beaches, unable to escape from water that has, in dramatic episodes, become seasonally depleted of oxygen over the past two decades.

Much of the conversation around our climate crisis highlights the emission of greenhouse gases and their effect on warming, precipitation, sea-level rise and ocean acidification. We hear little about the effect of climate change on oxygen levels, particularly in oceans and lakes. But water without adequate oxygen cannot support life, and for the three billion people who depend on coastal fisheries for income, declining ocean oxygen levels are catastrophic.

As ocean and atmospheric scientists focused on climate, we believe that oceanic oxygen levels are the next big casualty of global warming. To stop the situation from worsening, we need to expand our attention to include the perilous state of oceanic oxygen levels—the life-support system of our planet. We need to accelerate ocean-based climate solutions that boost oxygen, including nature-based solutions such as those discussed at the 2021 United Nations Climate Change Conference (COP26) held in Glasgow.

As the amount of carbon dioxide increases in the atmosphere, not only does it warm air by trapping radiation, it warms water. The interplay between oceans and the atmosphere is complex, but to put it simply, oceans have taken up about 90 percent of the excess heat created by climate change during the Anthropocene. Bodies of water can also absorb CO_2 and oxygen but only up to a limit: warmer water holds less oxygen. This decrease in oxygen content, coupled with a large-scale die-off of oxygen-generating phytoplankton resulting not just from climate change but from plastic pollution and industrial runoff, compromises ecosystems, asphyxiating marine life and leading to further die-offs. Large swaths of the oceans have lost 10 to 40 percent of their oxygen, and that loss is expected to accelerate with climate change.

The dramatic loss of oxygen from our bodies of water is compounding climate-related feedback mechanisms described by scientists in many fields, hundreds of whom signed the 2018 Kiel Declaration on Ocean Deoxygenation. This declaration has culminated in the new Global Ocean Oxygen Decade, a project under the U.N. Ocean Decade (2021–2030). Yet despite years of research into climate change and its effect on temperature, we know comparatively little about its effect on oxygen levels and what falling oxygen levels, in turn, may do to the wider earth system.

As the financial world invests in climate change solutions, possibly including future geoengineering efforts such as iron fertilization, we run the risk of exacerbating oxygen loss. We need to evaluate potential unintended consequences of climate solutions for the full life-support system.

Beyond enhanced monitoring of oxygen and the establishment of an oxygen-accounting system, such an agenda encompasses fully valuing the ecosystem co-benefits of carbon sequestration by our ocean's seaweed, seagrasses, mangroves and other wetlands. These so-called blue carbon nature-based solutions are also remarkable at oxygenating our planet through photosynthesis. At COP26 we saw a lot of primarily terrestrial initiatives and commitments, such as for forestry management, that are excellent steps forward. We hope the 2021 climate conference and this year's COP27 meeting help oceanic nature-based solutions to come into their own, propelled by the U.N. Ocean Decade.

Putting oxygen into the climate story motivates us to do the work to understand the deep systemic changes happening in our complex atmospheric and oceanic systems. Even as we celebrated the return of humpback whales in recent years to an increasingly clean New York Harbor and Hudson River, dead fish clogged the Hudson in the summer as warmer waters carried less oxygen. Ecosystem changes connected to physical and chemical systems-level data may point the way to new approaches to climate solutions–ones that encompass an enhanced understanding of the life-support system of our planet and complement our understanding of drawdown to reduce emissions of CO_2. Roughly 40 percent of the world's people depend on the ocean for their livelihoods. If we do not save marine life from oxygen starvation, we starve ourselves.

About the Authors

Nathalie Goodkin is a chemical oceanographer and an associate curator at the American Museum of Natural History.

Julie Pullen leads initiatives in climate risk and climate solutions. She is an adjunct research scientist at Columbia University's Earth Institute.

Scientists Are Taking Extreme Steps to Help Corals Survive

By Rebecca Albright

I'm standing on a beach in Australia, toes digging into the sand, zipping up my wet suit before I dive down to the Great Barrier Reef. As I stare out at the ocean, I'm excited by memories of my previous dive at this site a decade earlier. Growing up in Ohio, I had spent my childhood reading *A Day in the Life of a Marine Biologist* when I wasn't glued to the Discovery Channel. I got certified for scuba diving in one of Ohio's murky limestone quarries and made it to the Great Barrier Reef a year later. I'm remembering the anticipation squeezing my chest the day of that dive. My friend Emily, now an expert in marine algae, and I took bets on how long we could make our air last, which turned out to be about two magical hours. We were mesmerized by a forest of vibrant corals teaming with cuttlefish, giant purple clams and graceful sea turtles.

Now I am back, this time as a postdoctoral researcher at the Australian Institute of Marine Science. I wade in up to my chin, tip my head underwater and look through my mask. My heart drops. Gone are the cuttlefish. Gone are the giant clams. Gone are the turtles. The corals are drab. Most of the thriving life has been replaced by algae and sediment. Although I know senior scientists who shared gut-wrenching stories of how a particular reef had degraded over their long careers, I feel I am too young–barely 10 years in–to see this alarming degree of change. Shouldn't I be having this experience at the end of my tenure, not the beginning? Or better yet, not at all?

My shocked realization happened in 2014, as the third global mass-bleaching event began. Corals, often mistaken for rocks, are made of living animal tissue that contains microscopic algae, which provide the organism with food and give it color. When rising ocean temperature stresses corals, they expel the algae, causing the tissue to bleach–turn white–and leaving it vulnerable to starvation and disease. The mass bleaching persisted for three years, ruining reefs and breaking hearts worldwide. Although coral reefs can be threatened by overfishing, pollution and ocean acidification, the rapid and widespread destruction from warming is the greatest concern today.

The first major global bleaching events hit in 1998 and 2010, each time triggered by warming seas worsened by El Niño conditions. The 2014–2017 event was by far the longest and most extensive, harming more than 70 percent of the world's coral reefs. Two thirds of the Great Barrier Reef were reported as dead or severely bleached, and the devastating effects continue. Reefs are disappearing before our eyes. In the past 30 years we have lost around 50 percent of corals globally, and a recent report released by the United Nations's Intergovernmental Panel on Climate Change (IPCC) estimates we're at risk of losing more than 90 percent of coral reefs by 2050. We need solutions, and we need them fast.

Although reefs cover just 0.1 percent of the ocean floor, they support nearly 25 percent of all marine species, including fisheries that feed millions of people worldwide. They also provide natural breakwaters that protect coastal communities by reducing wave energy by up to 97 percent and wave height by up to 84 percent. And they generate vast tourism revenue. If we lose reefs, we jeopardize the livelihoods of 500 million people and more than $30 billion annually in goods and services. Even if you do not directly benefit from coral reefs, their destruction touches a chord in many people. As my colleague Luiz Rocha of the California Academy of Sciences puts it, "I may never live to see the *Mona Lisa*, but I still wouldn't want it to burn."

Driven by urgency, scientists are trying increasingly bold and creative ways to conserve and restore reef ecosystems. We are looking for techniques that are scalable and will not break the bank. Right now we are focusing on a handful of options that build on one another and can be integrated, including natural processes and human assistance. Together the steps might give corals the chance they need to make it through the coming decades, after which, it is hoped, the world will have drastically reduced its emissions, so warming will slow down.

I'm frequently asked: Will coral reefs survive? I think the answer is that they are resilient and might be able to cope, but they need breathing room—now.

Nursing Corals Back to Health

If you were to dive some seven kilometers off the coast of Florida, you might happen on one of several underwater forests of plastic trees with corals suspended from branches, like ornaments decorating a Christmas tree. Researchers are using such nurseries, as well as ones on land, to grow corals that can then be transplanted, or "outplanted," onto degraded reefs. Nurseries take advantage of the fact that all corals can reproduce sexually and asexually. Corals are clonal organisms—animals that are made up of hundreds to thousands of genetically identical polyps that are all clones of one another. They can reproduce sexually by creating eggs and sperm that fuse to create larvae and asexually when one polyp buds another.

When a coral is damaged by a storm, a piece of a colony might break off, tumble away, and eventually reattach to the bottom and continue to grow by cloning itself. Nursery practitioners can therefore deliberately fragment corals to create genetically identical clones. Today almost 90 species are successfully farmed around the world. Practitioners in the Caribbean and western Atlantic now grow and outplant tens of thousands of corals onto degraded reefs every year, often funded by private donors, grants or government restoration projects.

Scientists are looking to ramp up this restoration. About 14 years ago Dave Vaughan worked at Mote Coral Restoration. The techniques the researchers relied on then produced 600 corals in six years. The price tag on a single coral was about $1,000. But he discovered that because of a natural healing response, corals that are broken into tiny, eraser-size "micro fragments" can grow 25 to 50 times more quickly than corals in the wild. If pieces with the same genetic makeup (from the same parent) are placed a few centimeters apart, they will reconnect into a larger colony.

Now Erinn Muller, science director of Mote, says that the team can grow those 600 corals in an afternoon and has succeeded with all the half a dozen species it has tried; they are operating at less than $100 per coral, with some species costing only $25 per coral. By integrating citizen scientists and volunteers, Mote is convinced it can drop well below that number. The team can grow football-size corals that would have taken years to grow in the wild. Mote intends to produce and outplant up to 20,000 corals each year and grow this effort in years to come. Although the U.S. National Marine Fisheries Service says recovering the endangered Caribbean staghorn and elkhorn corals will require a minimum of $255 million and 400 years, Vaughan, who now works at Plant a Million Corals in Florida, hopes to remove them from the endangered species list in his lifetime.

We're now very good at growing corals and can, in many cases, successfully restore reefs to their historical range and function—at the local level. But a jump to the ecosystem level is massive. One of the toughest challenges is how to meaningfully scale restoration efforts to the big leagues. Most efforts cover less than a hectare, whereas reef degradation is occurring over hundreds to thousands of square kilometers. The price tag to replant the extensive Great Barrier Reef system, 2,300 kilometers in length, has been estimated at nearly $200 billion, using fragments at $5 apiece. But even that cost could be well worth it because the recovery would restore large fisheries that feed many people, create many jobs, and protect valuable coastlines and communities from storms.

Coral Sex

Along with growing corals asexually in nurseries, scientists are having increasing success in helping corals reproduce sexually, which can broaden genetic variation. As populations decline, genetic diversity is lost, which lessens corals' ability to resist warming water. Many Caribbean reefs, for example, are dominated by a single clone, and both science and history teach us that relying on low genetic variation, particularly in times of environmental change, can lead to disaster. In the 1800s, for example, a single clone of the Irish lumper potato fed Ireland's growing population until a rot wiped it out, devastating the island's people and economy. A more diverse crop would have fared much better. As in potatoes and people, genetic diversity can make corals less susceptible to environmental stress.

Sexual reproduction is nature's way of building diversity. Corals are fixed to the ocean floor, so they cannot move around in search of a mate. To reproduce sexually, most corals release eggs and sperm into the water column where, fingers crossed, fertilization happens. In degraded areas, where corals are few and far between, this becomes increasingly unlikely.

At the California Academy of Sciences, we are partnering with The Nature Conservancy and Secore International, a coral conservation organization, to help shepherd corals through this tricky process. We now have a good idea of when different coral species spawn. On predicted nights of spawning—after sunset, near a full moon in late summer (corals are surprisingly romantic)—coral colonies release eggs and sperm. We descend into the water with nets to harvest them and transfer these gametes to the laboratory, where we fertilize them in buckets of seawater. The resulting larvae are generally the size of sesame seeds and are vulnerable to being eaten in the wild until they settle and start to grow, so we raise them until they are big and healthy enough to be outplanted onto the reef. The goal is not to replant entire reefs but to maximize genetic variation and to rebuild enough of the population so the reef can recover naturally and be more resilient to the environment.

Many reefs have low genetic diversity, preventing them from churning out coral babies. By combining asexual and sexual restoration techniques, we may be able to restore one reef to the point where it can rebuild healthy reefs nearby. The aim is to create something that has a life beyond itself.

In the wild, only about one in a million coral babies survive. We are doing everything we can to help them through the vulnerable early stages. We can now achieve almost 100 percent success in fertilizing corals in the lab and settling the larvae onto tiles that can be outplanted, increasing the number of sexually compatible individuals that can improve future reproduction without our help. At a spawning event in Curaçao in the Caribbean in 2017, I helped a team collect five million eggs from 25 colonies within two short days. This is a new record for SECORE "and shows the scales we could work with," says the organization's founder Dirk Petersen.

In addition to helping corals reproduce in the wild, a handful of groups have started trying to spawn corals in public aquaria.

Worst Bleaching on Record

Relentlessly warm ocean water from 2014 to 2017 created the most extensive coral bleaching ever recorded. More than 70 percent of the earth's coral reefs were harmed. In 2016 alone (*map*), severe conditions spanned the globe (*white regions*). Hot water stresses corals, causing them to force algae out of their tissue, cutting off their food supply and leading to emaciation or death.

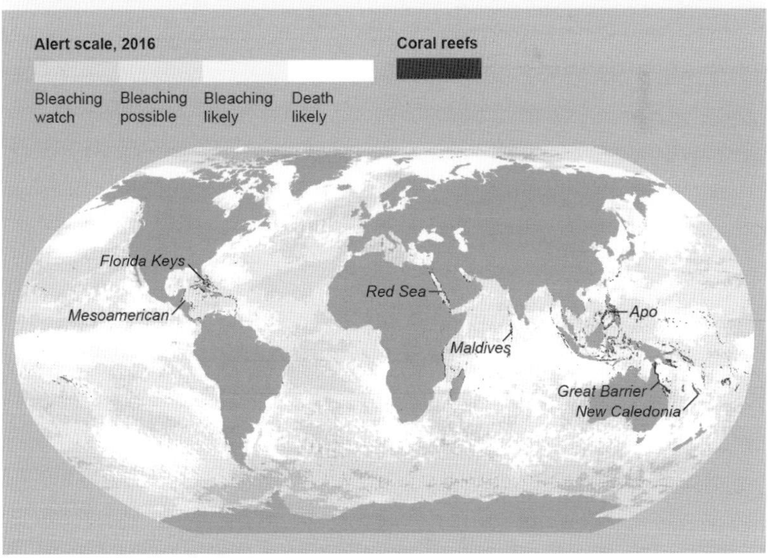

Credit: Mapping Specialists;
Source: NOAA Satellite and Information Service

No small feat, as it depends on our ability to mimic the suite of environmental cues that trigger reproduction, including lunar and seasonal cycles. Luckily, technological advances in aquaria-control systems are making it possible. At the California Academy of Sciences, I lead a team that has achieved two successful coral-spawning events—an accomplishment achieved in only one other location worldwide, the Horniman Museum in London. Our goal is to use this system to better understand the fundamental biology underlying coral reproduction and develop and validate methods that will help scale restoration efforts in the wild.

One of the biggest hurdles is keeping baby corals alive once we place them back in the sea. After all, degrading conditions are the main cause of coral decline in the first place, so until we tackle climate change, pollution and overfishing—via policy, awareness and global changes to the way we live—we are basically using a Band-Aid approach to buy reefs more time to try to survive. Along the way, we may be lucky enough to create genotypes through sexual reproduction that we could mass-produce with asexual techniques. We could then outplant them so Mother Nature could select which species might thrive.

Supercorals

We can't depend on good fortune for that scenario to happen. And because the ocean environment is changing too rapidly for many corals to adapt naturally, scientists are exploring other ways to accelerate the pace of adaptation. One approach is human-assisted evolution—enhancing traits that boost the capacity of corals, among other reef organisms, to tolerate stress and recover after bleaching events. Human-assisted evolution already surrounds our everyday lives. Most of the food we buy has been selectively bred or modified in some way (think "disease-resistant tomatoes"). Our pets have been selectively bred for certain aesthetics and personality traits. So why not breed or enhance corals to resist climate change?

Madeleine van Oppen of the Australian Institute of Marine Science and the Gates Coral Lab, directed by the late Ruth Gates, of the Hawaii Institute of Marine Biology are collaborating to enhance stress resistance. The Gates lab put corals on "environmental treadmills" to condition them to handle stress. Exposing certain corals in the lab to sublethal temperature stress may actually prompt them to turn on certain genes that help them better handle greater thermal stress in the long run. This process, known as epigenetic tuning, might be even more exciting if the trained corals are transplanted onto reefs, where they can transfer this ability to offspring, creating a generation of "supercorals." In theory, epigenetic tuning could enhance corals' ability to resist bleaching.

We are only beginning to understand this process. Early lab tests are promising, but field trials have yet to be conducted. Once done, they will reveal whether transplanted corals confer enhanced abilities to subsequent generations, whether the approach can be scaled up and at what cost, and whether any inherent risks exist.

Van Oppen is exploring selective breeding. A certain amount of genetic diversity exists within each species, leaving some of them more or less resistant to bleaching or disease. As breeders do with pets to optimize desired traits, if we can identify resistant coral colonies and breed them to produce resistant offspring, we may be able to improve the temperature tolerance of an entire reef as subsequent generations pass down the useful genes.

Breeding corals is difficult because they can take up to a decade to fully mature. Adapting to environmental change is hard for the same reason. But microbes and algae that live in symbiosis with corals typically mature rapidly and can influence a coral's health tremendously. We are thus trying to manipulate these organisms via artificial selection in ways that boost coral health. In recent years scientists have realized just how much our microbiome (the bacterial communities inside our body) influences our health, for better, for worse. Probiotics are now available in everything from yogurt to kombucha tea and even chocolate, claiming to boost digestion, immune function and overall health.

Van Oppen is now developing strains of algae in the lab and inoculating baby corals with them to see whether they confer thermal tolerance. She and the Gates lab have also been attempting to see if epigenetic tuning, selective breeding and microbiome manipulations done on the same corals could possibly be even more effective in combination.

It is still early days for most of the techniques we are trying. But some evidence suggests that they could be combined for even greater success. This approach might look like the following: First, we would use sexual reproduction and assisted evolution to generate improved and new diversity among coral populations and to create individuals that have greater stress tolerance. Then we would mass-produce them in nurseries using asexual techniques and outplant them to reefs.

Could this happen soon? Not exactly. Some techniques, such as selective breeding, are immediately tractable, inexpensive and effective. But more work is needed to establish the viability and scalability of other techniques and to gauge the risks of unanticipated ecological consequences. It is possible, for example, that artificially enhanced organisms might possess novel traits that allow them to outcompete native populations rather than integrating with them, which would undermine the very goal of helping reefs thrive. It is also possible, however, that the risk of doing nothing could be far worse.

Frozen for the Future

Whether we boost corals using single or combined techniques, one other step is vital: preserving sperm, eggs, larvae and entire coral fragments in the equivalent of seed banks, which agronomists have used for decades to help raise crop yields, disease resistance and drought tolerance. The banks allow researchers to pull out biological bits and pieces as needed to further improve resilience and diversity.

Taking a page from the in vitro fertilization (IVF) handbook, Mary Hagedorn of the Smithsonian Conservation Biology Institute has established the first genome repository for endangered coral species. In IVF, sperm or eggs are cooled with liquid nitrogen to extremely low temperatures. The eggs can be thawed, fertilized in the lab and transferred to the uterus as embryos. Originally developed for humans, the cryopreservation concept has spread to help endangered species worldwide.

In 2004, some years after the first human baby generated from a cryopreserved egg was born, Hagedorn created the coral cryoconservation program. Her team has developed a freezing system for sperm that can be applied to a wide range of coral species. To date, the team has successfully banked 16 species from around the world (2 percent of the earth's estimated 800 species). Thawed sperm have fertilization rates comparable to fresh sperm, and the resulting embryos develop normally into healthy juveniles.

Hagedorn has distributed this germplasm, or living tissue, to cryobanks in various countries. Theoretically, it could remain frozen and alive for hundreds to thousands of years. The germ line cells could later be thawed and used in natural and captive breeding programs. For example, frozen sperm could fertilize eggs from places far beyond the sperm's natural range, introducing new genes into the coral gene pool. And of course, the banks can preserve species that may decline or disappear if reefs collapse.

Hagedorn hopes to cryopreserve eggs (in addition to sperm) and whole larvae before moving on to entire micro fragments. She is also developing techniques to cryopreserve fish testes to help conserve reef-fish biodiversity. Ultimately she envisions a future in which the germplasms of corals and other endangered reef organisms are deposited in highly secure facilities, making eggs, sperm and embryos available to broaden genetic diversity and rebuild reefs. "We have no idea what science will be able to do in 100 years," Hagedorn says.

Where do we go from here? Although some of these solutions may seem too unconventional by today's standards, we must invest in strategies for tomorrow. Many of these techniques have yet to be tested beyond the conceptual or lab stage, and questions remain about the scalability, costs and ecological consequences of manipulating reef systems. The consequences of doing nothing, however, threaten corals and the many species that rely on them.

What we know for sure is that there is no single fix to the problems plaguing coral reefs. Scientists are throwing everything they have at different options to buy reefs time. Although none of today's techniques is likely to salvage reefs at the global scale, many show promise on local or regional levels. The reefs of tomorrow may not resemble the reefs of today, but they can still provide important goods and services to ecosystems and to people. Climate change, pollution and overfishing are the larger challenges. We have to tackle them collectively to protect oceans overall and give coral reefs the breathing room they need to survive.

Referenced

Global Warming and Recurrent Mass Bleaching of Corals. Terry P. Hughes et al. in *Nature*, Vol. 543, pages 373–377; March 16, 2017.

California Academy of Sciences' reef program: www.calacademy.org/explore-science/hope-for-reefs

Mote Marine Laboratory's micro fragment program: https://mote.org/research/program/coral-reef-restoration

Secore International's coral conservation program: www.secore.org

About the Author

Rebecca Albright is a coral biologist and curator at the California Academy of Sciences. She focuses on how coral reef ecosystems cope with changing environmental conditions.

Australia's Angry Summer: This Is What Climate Change Looks Like

By Nerilie Abram

Summer in Australia use to be something we yearned for: long, lazy days spent by the beach or pool, backyard barbecues, and games of cricket with family and friends. But recent summers have become a time of fear: Schools and workplaces are closed because of catastrophic fire danger, while we shelter in air-conditioned spaces to avoid dangerous heat waves and hazardous levels of smoke in the air. Campgrounds have been closed for the summer, and entire towns have been urged to evacuate ahead of "Code Red" fire weather. Welcome to our new climate.

Of course, unusually hot summers have happened in the past; so have bad bushfire seasons. But the link between the current extremes and anthropogenic climate change is scientifically undisputable.

The fires raging across the southern half of the Australian continent this year have so far burned through more than 5 million hectares. To put that in context, the catastrophic 2018 fire season in California saw nearly 740,000 hectares burned. The Australian fire season began this year in late August (before the end of our winter). Fires have so far claimed nine lives, including two firefighters, and destroyed around 1,000 homes. It is too early to tell what the toll on our wildlife has been, but early estimates suggest that around 500 million animals have died so far, including 30 percent of the koala population in their main habitat. And this is all before we have even reached January and February, when the fire season typically peaks in Australia.

Australia is the most fire prone of all of Earth's continents. But what has made its latest fire season so extreme? Wildfires need four ingredients: available fuel, dryness of that fuel, weather conditions that aid the rapid spread of fire and an ignition. Climate change is making Australian wildfires larger and more frequent because of its effects on dryness and fire weather.

Australia's climate has warmed by more than one degree Celsius over the past century, and this change has caused an increase in the frequency and intensity of heat waves. I am 42, and I have lived through only six years with average temperatures below the 1961–1990 climatological average. My children have experienced none, and in all likelihood, they never will.

Increasing temperatures cause increased evaporation that dries the soil and fuel load. More than a decade ago, the Intergovernmental Panel on Climate Change (IPCC) concluded that ongoing anthropogenic climate change was virtually certain to increase the intensity and frequency of fires in Australia. This assessment of the science evidence has been repeated in countless reports, including the IPCC's *Climate Change and Land* report, released in August 2019.

The effects of rising temperature on drying out the environment can be countered by rainfall or by the growth of vegetation that increases humidity locally. But in the southern half of Australia, where rain falls mostly in the winter, there has been a substantial decline in precipitation. In the southwest of the country, rainfall has declined by around 20 percent since the 1970s, and in the southeast, around 11 percent of rainfall has been lost since the 1990s.

One of the factors driving this long-term loss of winter rainfall is the positive trend in the Southern Annular Mode (SAM). This change is causing the westerly winds that circle the Southern Ocean to shift southward toward Antarctica, causing rain-bearing winter cold fronts to pass south of the Australian continent. The role of anthropogenic climate change in driving this trend in the SAM is also clear in the science.

Climate variability acts on top of these long-term trends that are pushing the Australian climate toward a more fire-prone state. And that variability is an important part of the story of why the 2019–2020 summer has been so extreme.

Southeastern Australia has been in drought since 2017. Rainfall here is normally highly variable from year to year, but there have now been three winters in a row where the winter rains failed. This is a situation that has never been seen before in the historical record of Australia's rainfall, even during infamous decade-long droughts such as the Millennium Drought. The severity of the current drought has caused large swathes of vegetation to die. It has even dried out wet rain forests, allowing fierce fires to take hold in places that would not normally burn.

The current summer has presented the perfect storm for wildfire. Long-term climate warming, combined with years of drought, colliding with a set of climate patterns that deliver severe fire weather.

In the tropical Indian Ocean, one of the most severe positive Indian Ocean Dipole (IOD) events on record played out this year. The unusually cold sea-surface temperatures in the eastern Indian Ocean cut off one of Australia's critical moisture sources, adding to the ongoing drought in southern parts of the country. Australia's worst fire seasons typically follow positive IOD events, much more so than the influence of El Niño events in the Pacific. Again, climate change is part of the story, because anthropogenic warming is causing positive IOD events to become stronger and more frequent.

At the same time, this year, a rare sudden stratospheric warming event developed over the Antarctic in late winter. Weakening of the polar vortex over Antarctica in spring increases the forest fire danger index across eastern Australia. This is because a northward shift in the Southern Hemisphere westerlies (i.e., a negative SAM) at this time of year causes very hot and dry westerly winds to be drawn across the continent.

The angry summer playing out in Australia right now was predictable. The scientific evidence is well known for how anthropogenic greenhouse gas emissions are causing long-term climate change and altering climate variability in ways that increase our fire risk. The role of climate change in the unprecedented fires gripping Australia is also well understood by our emergency services. Sadly, though, this summer has occurred against a backdrop in which the Australian government has argued, on the world stage, to scale back our greenhouse-gas-emissions-reduction targets. Our leaders are literally fiddling while the country burns.

In many parts of Australia, there will be no traditional fireworks shows to welcome in the new year. The risk is simply too great, and celebration is not warranted while our communities continue to be under threat from this angry summer.

This was originally published as an opinion piece. The views expressed are those of the author(s) and are not necessarily those of Scientific American.

About the Author

Nerilie Abram is an investigator at the ARC Center of Excellence for Climate Extremes and an associate professor at the Research School of Earth Sciences at the Australian National University.

Yes, Climate Change Is Making Severe Weather Worse

By Jennifer Francis

She was born in the usual way. A disorganized blob of clouds emerged over the Atlantic Ocean off Africa's bulging western coast, just north of the equator. Atmospheric pressure there was low, typical for late summer. Natural variability in the earth's climate spawns tropical disturbances every year in this area—sometimes more, sometimes fewer, and sometimes they become hurricanes. Weather forecast models unanimously predicted that the clouds would coalesce into a storm that curved harmlessly northwest into the mid-Atlantic, far from land.

On September 1, 2018, tropical storm Florence began to do just that but then turned stubbornly westward while becoming better organized, seemingly aimed at the Caribbean. Another worrisome disturbance was already lurking near Puerto Rico, which was still reeling from Hurricane Maria's devastation a year before. Three major cyclones were also spinning in the tropical Pacific, fueled by ocean temperatures that were off the charts. The mob of storms drew energy from record-warm ocean temperatures, which have risen steadily since the 1970s in lockstep with increasing atmospheric temperatures, driven by heat-trapping greenhouse gases—global effects of climate change. Storms feed of ocean heat and water vapor in the atmosphere, which is climbing as well.

Conflicting factors kept Florence weak, however. Although that seemed fortunate, it provoked anxiety among forecasters. Weaker storms are more readily steered by lower-altitude winds, and those winds were blowing east to west, straight at the U.S. East Coast. They were skirting the southern rim of a big, circular, unusually strong high-pressure center parked in the middle of the North Atlantic. High-pressure centers arise naturally, but evidence shows that some are getting stuck in place more often, a regional symptom of a warmer climate. A "blocking high" like this one had steered Hurricane Sandy on its bizarre path from the Atlantic into New Jersey in 2012.

On September 4 something unexpected happened: weak Florence moved over a spot in the west-central Atlantic that was abnormally warm. Fueled by that warmth, she rapidly intensified to a Category 4 hurricane and at a nearly record-breaking northerly latitude. Random hot pools of ocean water are another regional effect of our changing climate.

As Florence churned, the forecast models began to coalesce: she seemed likely to hit the coastal Carolinas and stall, where she could unleash deep flooding as Hurricane Harvey had done a year earlier over Houston. Sure enough, Florence struck the coastal Carolinas on September 14 and sat for four days. The low-altitude steering winds were now too weak to move the system. Florence dropped more than 30 inches of rain in places and reportedly killed more than 50 people and millions of animals (mostly chickens) while racking up an estimated $20 billion or so in losses. Floodwaters passing through factory farms, mines and sewage-treatment plants polluted rivers and estuaries for weeks.

Florence's wrath will not soon be forgotten, and neither will the blatant demonstration of climate change in action. The hurricane's unusual severity can be attributed to specific effects of climate change: greater heat in the air and ocean, extra water vapor, the tenacious blocking high and weak steering winds. These factors are in play around the world, favoring rapid storm intensification, heavier precipitation, greater flooding and stronger storm winds.

Florence was just one of many examples in 2018 of the various ways climate change is afecting extreme weather. Multiple "bomb cyclones" battered the northeastern U.S. An outbreak of Arctic air called the "beast from the east" froze Europe. Severe heat waves crippled Japan, Scandinavia and Greece. Floods ruined parts of Venice, Paris and Maryland.

Such misfortunes have happened since humans walked the earth, of course. But every year it becomes clearer that today's epidemic of bizarre weather cannot be explained by natural variability. Although in the past scientists were careful to not directly link climate change to specific weather events, we are now indeed saying that because of climate change, major floods are occurring more often. Killer heat waves are hotter and lasting longer. Cold spells are sticking around longer in some places, too.

How much of our daily wild weather, which in 2018 caused more than $160 billion in losses worldwide, can be blamed on changing climate? The answer depends on untangling the roles of three broad factors. First is the global effect of more heat in the ocean and more heat and vapor in the atmosphere. The water vapor story deserves more attention than it gets: vapor is another greenhouse gas that traps heat, it releases even more heat when it condenses into clouds, and it feeds precipitation from storms.

The second factor is regional effects, such as stubborn, blocking high-pressure centers, expanses of melting sea ice, a growing "cold blob" of ocean water south of Greenland, a slowing Gulf Stream and an increasingly disrupted polar vortex.

The third involves the complicated ways that natural variations, such as El Niño and La Niña, interact with the regional factors. Research into this interplay is cutting-edge, controversial–and bearing fruit. We now understand better how and why climate change is escalating extreme weather, revealing how we will need to prepare for increasingly frequent and intense dangers.

A Nasty Nor'Easter

The earth's atmosphere is a cloak of roiling gases. Air constantly heats and cools, with the sun pouring in energy during the day and warm surfaces radiating it back to space at night. Uneven heating creates local winds that blow every which way. Water is continuously evaporating from land and sea, condensing in the air and falling down as rain or snow.

Yet within this chaos are remarkably predictable patterns governed by latitude, the earth's spin, mountain ranges, ocean circulations and other influences. In the Atlantic, hurricanes like Florence form in the eastern tropics and move westward. In the Pacific, tropical storms move westward, too. A polar jet stream blows from west to east around the Northern Hemisphere at a latitude near the U.S.-Canada border; another polar jet in the Southern Hemisphere crosses the lower reaches of South America and Africa. More cyclical are large wind systems linked to ocean-temperature fluctuations, such as El Niño and La Niña, which wax and wane every three to eight years and affect winds and precipitation worldwide. Data from cores of mud extracted from various seabeds show these patterns have held for hundreds of thousands of years.

Chaos and consistency also prevail in the oceans, over longer cycles, amid constant heating, cooling and flowing waters. The Pacific Decadal Oscillation is a seesawing of warm and cold temperatures between the eastern and western North Pacific Ocean, each phase persisting for about a decade. The Atlantic Meridional Overturning Circulation is a slow current of warm, salty surface water that heads north in the western Atlantic, then loses heat, dives deep and flows back south to Antarctica. A round-trip through this circuit takes about 1,000 years.

Interactions between the atmosphere and oceans introduce natural variability into climate. Some years are hotter or colder in certain regions; some years are wetter or drier. But those same mud-core data from past millennia show that the variability has limits: the climate rarely exceeds certain bounds. Until now.

I experienced one of those exceptions firsthand in the late winter of 2018. March is supposed to roar in like a lion, but this was ridiculous. Mother Nature was delivering a parade of potent nor'easters–storms that churn just off the Atlantic Coast, lashing the Eastern Seaboard with winds from the northeast. The three climate change factors–higher heat and vapor globally, regional effects, and the interplay between natural variability and those effects–are goosing these storms.

I was anxiously monitoring the latest forecast models. They showed a seemingly innocuous wiggle in the jet stream over the

North Pacific, and they agreed that it would cross to the Atlantic Seaboard and spawn a whopper of a storm aimed at our coastal town in southeastern Massachusetts. The models were bullish about a blizzard developing quickly–technically a bomb cyclone–and dumping its snow right on my neighborhood. It would be the third major nor'easter of the season, which is unusual.

All the ingredients were in place. Cold air was entrenched over Eastern states (a naturally occurring factor). Extra heat in the ocean (a global factor) provided ample energy and moisture for a mounting storm. Water temperatures in the Atlantic off New England were far above normal (a regional factor).

The interplay between natural and regional factors was another important ingredient. In late 2013 the Pacific Decadal Oscillation flipped from its so-called negative phase to a positive phase, in keeping with its natural cycle. It raised sea temperatures above average along the western coast of North America. Extra heat pumped into the atmosphere from this warm water favors the formation of a northward bulge (called a ridge) in the jet stream over western North America that can extend into Alaska.

That is where interaction with a regional effect comes into play. Air temperatures in the Arctic have risen two to three times faster than the rest of the planet, especially in winter. The extraordinary loss of 75 percent of the Arctic's sea-ice volume in only 40 years is responsible for most of this warming. The Pacific ridge can tap into this extra warmth, causing it to intensify and stick around for a long time. This so-called Ridiculously Resilient Ridge is largely responsible for the extended drought and heat waves that set the stage for recent severe wildfires along the U.S. West Coast.

A strong ridge is usually accompanied by a large southward dip (called a trough) to the east of it, which in this case was over eastern North America. A deep trough allows cold Arctic air to plunge far southward, creating a stark temperature contrast with the warm Atlantic waters along the East Coast. The atmosphere despises temperature contrasts. It generates storms to mix air masses in an attempt to even out the differences; bomb cyclones are an intense example of this process. This ridge-and-trough pattern tends to spawn nor'easters, and it has become increasingly prevalent in recent winters.

Sure enough, National Weather Service data painted a scenario of "bombogenesis"—when a storm's atmospheric pressure drops more than 24 millibars in 24 hours, causing it to "explode" in size and power. My neighborhood was in the crosshairs. As dusk arrived on March 2, so did the nor'easter's howling wind, driving rain and snow, power outages, and major erosion from high waves and storm surges. Afraid that one of the tall white pines in our yard might fall on the house, my cat and I (my husband was away) opted to sleep on the living-room couch rather than in my upstairs bedroom. The wind roared so loudly overnight that I did not hear the crash of any of the 20 big trees that dropped around us, somehow missing our roof.

The storm took its sweet time leaving, as a blocking high-pressure center near Greenland thwarted its movement, ravaging half a dozen states with hurricane-force winds. The nor'easter killed at least nine individuals, knocked out power for more than two million people (five days in our town) and flooded coastal communities.

Wicked Winter Weather

The parade of destructive nor'easters was not the only winter weather in 2018 juiced by climate change. Parisians and Venetians suffered the worst flooding in half a century as a result of prolonged rainfall, while deadly windstorms struck Germany and northern France. Several feet of snow buried Davos, Switzerland, just as the well-heeled and high-heeled tried to arrive for the annual meeting of the World Economic Forum.

In North America, the big story was "weather whiplash"—sudden and dramatic shifts between long-lasting extremes. Although research is still sparse, evidence is accumulating that these exaggerated swings are occurring more frequently and that our three climate influences are in play.

Case in point: during three weeks of January 2019, such bitter cold gripped the eastern U.S. that iguanas in southern Florida dropped from trees in near-frozen comas while residents in Western states basked in above-normal temperatures. Then in early February, weather whiplash struck. An abrupt reversal in the jet-stream pattern brought record-breaking warmth to hundreds of Eastern cities. Temperatures jumped more than 40 degrees Fahrenheit in 24 hours, bringing the iguanas back to life. At the same time, a deep chill settled over the Western states. In the atmospheric battleground between the eastern and western air masses, potent storms in the Mississippi Valley caused the worst flooding in decades. The frequency of heavy precipitation in that region has increased by about 40 percent since the 1950s.

Global, regional and interplay factors had struck again. Overall global warming and moistening certainly gave these extremes a boost. And the same regionally loopy jet stream that would contribute to the parade of bomb cyclones had set the stage. Winter whiplash slapped the U.S. and Canada in February 2019, too; in some areas, temperatures ricocheted by 50 or 60 degrees F and wind chills by more than 100 degrees F in only a few days.

Scorching, Soaking Summer

Summer 2018 also brought a smorgasbord of rough weather to the Northern Hemisphere, much of it exacerbated by climate change. While Japan, Texas and even Scandinavia baked for weeks, the U.S. Eastern Seaboard sloshed through its wettest season on record. Tenacious droughts plagued the western U.S., parts of Europe and the Middle East, contributing to a horrific spate of wildfires that cost $20 billion in California alone. Extreme summer conditions ruined crops, boosted toxic algae blooms, shut down nuclear-reactor cooling systems and triggered blackouts across four continents.

Some impacts were clearly related to the global factor. Higher average temperatures cause hotter heat waves. Extra water vapor feeds summer downpours and helps to raise nighttime temperatures by trapping additional heat near the surface. The exceptional heat plus humidity, especially at night, can be a deadly combination, making it difficult for the human body to cool itself through evaporation of sweat. Worldwide, thousands of people without air-conditioning died.

Less straightforward were climate influences on the summer jet stream–literally a "hot" research topic. What is already clear, though, is that both global and regional factors are involved in favoring an unusually wavy jet stream such as the one that engulfed Scandinavia in heat waves, drought and fire. Temperatures there from May through July in 2018 broke records going back 260 years.

What role did regional changes play? During spring and summer, warming occurs across a band of land south of Canada and Russia's Arctic coasts. Spring snow cover has been melting there ever earlier. The loss of this highly reflective surface exposes the underlying soil to strong spring sunshine sooner, drying it out earlier. Dry soil warms much faster than damp soil, so temperatures climb. The warm-up gives summer a head start, shifting the jet stream northward sooner than usual, allowing warm air to penetrate high latitudes.

The band of abnormally warm land can help split the jet stream into two branches, a common occurrence during winter but less so in summer. Weather systems between the two often get trapped for long periods because there is little wind there to move them along. During the summer of 2018 the jet stream over Eurasia and North America was split much of the time, creating persistently warm, dry conditions in some areas, and prolonged rainy periods in others, that broke records on both continents.

Fasten Your Seat Belt

The wild weather of 2018 was a trailer for the main feature, coming to audiences everywhere as greenhouse gases continue to accumulate. Some of the consequences of global effects–warmer oceans, warmer air and increased atmospheric moisture–are obvious and direct. Intense research is focused on untangling the jumble of regional effects and their interplay with natural variability. Let's look at four examples.

Evidence suggests that the earth's tropical zone around the equator has been widening toward the poles. That pushes storm tracks poleward and makes some temperate regions hotter and drier. The clearest symptoms can be seen in the dry zones that define the northern and southern edges of the tropics, such as southern California, the Mediterranean and Australia, where more severe droughts and heat waves have captured headlines. Scientists are working to understand the likely contributors–warming, atmospheric dust and soot particles that alter air temperatures and cloud formation.

Another regional factor under scrutiny is the apparent slowing of the Gulf Stream, a major ocean current flowing from the Gulf of Mexico up the Eastern Seaboard, then across the North Atlantic toward the U.K. It is the surface branch of the larger Atlantic Meridional Overturning Circulation. A slowdown would upset weather patterns and fisheries on both sides of the ocean. Measurements of the subsurface ocean are sparse, but oddities in well-monitored surface temperatures, such as abnormal warmth along the East Coast and the blob of cool waters south of Greenland, provide important clues that this large-scale circulation system may indeed be slowing. A shift in ocean-temperature patterns will alter the strength and path of storms. A hyperactive North Atlantic storm track in recent years may be a response to a slowing Gulf Stream, along with feverish waters that most likely fomented the bomb cyclones of the winter of 2018.

Blocking high-pressure centers are another regional feature to watch. Observations suggest they are occurring more often in some places, such as over Greenland and western Russia, but atmospheric models struggle to predict the development and demise of these swirling eddies in the sky. Blocks can form for various reasons, some related to natural variability and some to climate change. The remnants of tropical storms, for example, can naturally inject surges of energy into the jet stream, causing it to buckle and spin off orphan eddies. As oceans warm, however, tropical storms may survive farther northward and later into the autumn season, increasing the likelihood of collisions with the jet stream that can create a block, which can then push hurricanes and other weather systems in unusual directions.

During October 2018, for example, Hurricane Leslie dawdled in the Atlantic for more than two weeks, finally going where no known hurricane has gone before: just west of Portugal. Strong winds and flooding rains pummeled the Iberian Peninsula. At the time, a strong block sat over northeastern Europe, creating the wavy jet-stream pattern that captured Leslie and carried it on a long journey across the Atlantic.

A final regional factor is the stratospheric polar vortex, which was in the news frequently in the winter of 2018—and again in the winter of 2019. It has been behaving oddly. This ring of strong winds circles a pool of frigid air over the North Pole only in winter, at an altitude of around 30 miles. Every few years the right conditions can deform the ring or even split it into two or more smaller rings, which tend to migrate southward, bringing severe cold spells with them. Simultaneously, warm air from the south invades the Arctic, creating topsy-turvy temperatures. During the split polar vortex in late January 2019, it was warmer near the North Pole than in Chicago. These so-called sudden stratospheric warming events can occur naturally, but lately they are happening more often. Several new studies have found that the dramatic sea-ice loss in the Arctic Ocean north of western Russia may help trigger these vortex disruptions. Those of us living in the midlatitudes may be attacked more frequently by the polar vortex as global warming intensifies.

Although certain aspects of the uncontrolled experiment we are forcing on the earth's climate remain elusive, science is rapidly revealing that climate change can be blamed for amplifying extreme weather and its consequences. Understanding the links will help us see the future more clearly and prepare for the impacts on agriculture, international security, marine life, forests, freshwater resources, infrastructure and human health. The effects are already apparent and will only worsen.

Yet there is reason for hope. The rash of bad weather has shined a bright light on the well-funded campaign to spread disinformation and generate doubt about climate change among the public. Despite what the doubters say, natural variability simply cannot explain the extremes we already see and feel. Recent surveys show most people finally accept that climate change is real and caused by us. Insurers, military leaders, property developers and municipal administrators are responding to the tangible risks to life and property. Perhaps we are finally ready to confront the rough ride ahead.

Referenced

More-Persistent Weak Stratospheric Polar Vortex States Linked to Cold Extremes. Marlene Kretschmer et al. in *Bulletin of the American Meteorological Society*, Vol. 99, No. 1, pages 49-60; January 2018.

Observed Fingerprint of a Weakening Atlantic Ocean Overturning Circulation. L. Caesar et al. in *Nature*, Vol. 556, pages 191-196; April 12, 2018.

Re-examining Tropical Expansion. Paul W. Staten et al. in *Nature Climate Change*, Vol. 8, pages 768-775; September 2018.

About the Author

Jennifer Francis is a senior scientist at the Woods Hole | Research Center in Falmouth, Mass. She was a research professor at Rutgers University from 1994 to 2018. Francis serves on Scientific American*'s board of advisers.*

Section 3: Societal Impacts of Climate Change

3.1 The Unfolding Tragedy of Climate Change in Bangladesh
By Robert Glennon

3.2 How Climate Change Is Making It Harder to Predict Outbreaks
By Lois Parshley

3.3 Climate Change Hastened Syria's Civil War
By Mark Fischetti

3.4 Climate Change Is Creating New Vocabulary, from Eco-Anxiety to Kaitiakitanga
By Trish Stewart

3.5 How Cities Can Protect Themselves from Rising Waters
By Ziqian (Cecilia) Dong

The Unfolding Tragedy of Climate Change in Bangladesh

By Robert Glennon

In some places, the impact of climate change is obvious. In others, scientists predict that climate change will occur based on elaborate computer models. In Bangladesh, it is already happening at a scale that involves unprecedented human tragedy. I witnessed this in December 2016, when I visited Bangladesh to give some talks at the University of Chittagong.

December 9, 2016."How do they survive?" I kept wondering as I walked the alleys of Old Dhaka, the capital of Bangladesh, a country with a population of 164 million on a landmass the size of New York State. People seem to be everywhere in Dhaka, in a churning frenzy of rickshaws, CNGs (Compressed Natural Gas vehicles), taxis, buses, horse-drawn carriages and people–16 million and rapidly growing. The newest arrivals, mostly climate change refugees, end up in decrepit slums.

December 18, 2016. "What will the sea do next," I thought when I visited the remote village of Premasia, Bangladesh, at the junction of the Sangu River and the Bay of Bengal, south of Chittagong. The schoolchildren greeted us with spontaneous joyfulness, full of hope, despite the visible aftermath of Cyclone Roanu, which struck in May 2016, washing away homes and permanently ruining croplands from salt deposits. Their three-story concrete school, raised on stilts, served as a cyclone shelter during the storm. Isolated palm trees, now surrounded by water and beach, are haunting reminders that here once stood someone's home. Rising sea levels are turning land into sea bottom, driving some people farther inland. Others rebuild repeatedly, just as Sisyphus kept pushing the rock up the hill.

December 25, 2016. "Bare rock in the high Himalayas?" I gasped as my guide Phuri Kitar Sherpa pointed out Machapuchare, also known as Fish Tail, an immense obelisk of stone perched above

Pokhara, Nepal, a jumping off spot for trekkers and alpinists. A third-generation Sherpa guide, Phuri told me he rarely used to see bare stone on this holy site, now off limits to climbing and never summited. Climate change is responsible for a long-term decline in snowpack in the Himalayas, which exacerbates flooding in rivers that flow into Bangladesh.

One of the poorest countries on Earth, Bangladesh has made remarkable strides since gaining its independence in a war with Pakistan in 1971. On December 15, 2016, I met with A.B.M. Fazle Karim Chowdhury, a Member of Parliament, who explained, with a measure of pride, "once there was a shortage of food, now we export food." Bangladesh once led the world in child mortality. No longer. Due to better health care, life expectancy rose by 10 years, from 59 to 69 between 1990 and 2010. Providing free birth control empowered women and reduced the fertility rate from seven children per woman to three, which is substantially lowering population growth rates. Universal primary education is helping to create a more skilled workforce. Perhaps most impressive, the poverty rate declined from 57 percent to 25 percent between 1990 and 2014. With GNP rates annually hovering around seven percent, MP Chowdhury has reason to proclaim, "We are a developing country. Soon, we'll be a developed country."

In December 2016, construction seemed ubiquitous in Dhaka and Chittagong. Even the garment industry, which has a woeful record of protecting workers rights, made painfully obvious by the collapse of a factory in 2013, which killed more than 1,000 workers, shows signs of change. I visited Smart Jeans Ltd. on December 13, 2016. The factory's bright lights, spotlessly clean floors, and sophisticated air filtration system reminded me more of a hospital in the United States than a sweatshop in a developing country. However, the impact of climate change may overwhelm this progress.

Bangladesh sits at the head of the Bay of Bengal, astride the largest river delta on Earth, formed by the junction of the Brahmaputra, Ganges, and Meghna rivers. Nearly one-quarter of Bangladesh is less than seven feet above sea level; two-thirds of the country is less than 15 feet above sea level. Most Bangladeshis live along coastal areas where alluvial delta soils provide some of the best farmland in the country.

Sea surface temperatures in the shallow Bay of Bengal have significantly increased, which, scientists believe, has caused Bangladesh to suffer some of the fastest recorded sea level rises in the world. Storm surges from more frequent and stronger cyclones push walls of water 50 to 60 miles up the Delta's rivers.

At the same time, the melting of glaciers and snowpack in the Himalayas, which hold the third largest body of snow on Earth, has swollen the rivers that flow into Bangladesh from Tibet, Nepal, Bhutan, and India. So too have India's water policies. India diverts large quantities of water for irrigation during the dry season and releases most water during the monsoon season.

According to the Bangladesh government's 2009 Climate Change Strategy and Action Plan, "in an 'average' year, approximately one quarter of the country is inundated." Every four to five years, "there is a severe flood that may cover over 60% of the country." Rapid erosion of coastal areas has inundated dozens of islands in the Bay. For example, Sandwip Island, near Chittagong, has lost 90 percent of its original 23-square-miles–mostly in the last two decades.

Climate change in Bangladesh has started what may become the largest mass migration in human history. In recent years, riverbank erosion has annually displaced between 50,000 and 200,000 people. The population of what the Bangladesh government calls "immediately threatened" islands, called "chars," exceeds four million.

The Bangladesh riverine environment is so dynamic that, as chars wash away, the process of accretion creates new chars downstream. Land is so scarce and the population so dense that the displaced people try to eke out an existence on these new, highly unstable sand bars.

A three-foot rise in sea level would submerge almost 20 percent of the entire country and displace more than 30 million people. Some scientists project a five-to-six foot rise by 2100, which would displace perhaps 50 million people. As perspective, the ongoing tragedy in Syria has caused the exodus of approximately three million people.

Already, the intruding sea has contaminated groundwater, which supplies drinking water for coastal regions, and degraded farmland, rendering it less fertile and eventually barren.

It is not just people who are affected. The Sundarbans, the largest mangrove forest in the world and a World Heritage Site, lies in the delta of the Ganges River in Bangladesh and India. Home to the iconic Bengal tiger, the Sundarbans also play a critical role in protecting Bangladesh's coastal areas from storm surges caused by cyclones.

Nevertheless, across coastal Bangladesh, sea-level rise, exacerbated by the conversion of mangrove forest for agricultural production and shrimp farming, has resulted in the loss of hundreds of thousands of acres of mangroves. In the Sundarbans, the number of tigers has plummeted. The World Wildlife Fund predicts that the tiger may become extinct. Further loss of mangrove habitat, especially in the Sundarbans, also means that Bangladesh will lose one of its last natural defenses against climate change-induced super-cyclones.

Engineering adaptations to climate change that have been successful in other nations–such as the dikes constructed in the Netherlands–won't work in Bangladesh because the soils are sandy and constantly shifting. The government has undertaken measures to adapt to climate change. It has developed an effective early warning system to alert coastal rural areas of impending cyclones; built a network of 2,100 cyclone shelters, which can accommodate more than a million people; and financed 4,000 miles of coastal embankment projects. It is even planting trees on chars in an effort to create islands that are more durable. However, despite its economic progress, Bangladesh remains a poor country with limited resources. Some measures, such as levees made of sand bags along the Bay of Bengal and the Sangu River, may temporarily stem the ocean's advance, but they offer at best a short-term fix.

These changes are happening *to* the people of Bangladesh, not caused *by* them. As a country, Bangladesh emits only 0.3 percent of the emissions producing climate change.

February 16, 2017. "Where will they go?" Climate refugees, mostly rural farmers and fishermen, are moving into the slums of the country's two largest cities, Dhaka and Chittagong. As conditions deteriorate, the capacity of these areas to absorb more people is nearing the end. The sad reality offers limited options to those displaced. Climate refugees from Bangladesh, a predominantly Muslim country, are not welcome in the neighboring countries of India and Myanmar. India is building its version of a border wall, a barbed-wire fence; violence in Myanmar in December 2016 drove an estimated 65,000 Rohingya, an ethnic Muslim minority, into Bangladesh.

It is exceedingly unlikely that the Trump Administration either will welcome Bangladeshi refugees or provide financial support to underwrite costs of relocation to other countries. Opportunities for resettlement in the rest of the world are dwindling.

The unfolding calamity demands a response from the international community. Wealthy countries have generated most of the greenhouse gases that are harming Bangladesh. If these countries are unwilling to absorb tens of millions of refugees, there is a moral imperative for them to help. They should underwrite the adaptation efforts of the Bangladesh government and the construction of roads, power plants, water supply systems, housing and other infrastructure to allow these climate refugees to remain and thrive in their own country.

This was originally published as an opinion piece. The views expressed are those of the author(s) and are not necessarily those of Scientific American.

About the Author

Robert Glennon is a Regents' Professor at the University of Arizona College of Law and author of Unquenchable: America's Water Crisis *and* What to Do About It.

How Climate Change Is Making It Harder to Predict Outbreaks

By Lois Parshley

Kobus Steenkamp's farm sprawls along a dirt road in South Africa's central plains, where the sky makes everything seem small. Steenkamp woke up here one morning after the rains in 2010 to find something strange happening with his sheep. "You could see there's blood at their backs," he recalls. All his pregnant ewes were losing their lambs.

It was every farmer's nightmare: his herd had been infected by Rift Valley fever, a mosquito-borne virus that causes abortion and death in livestock and wildlife and can be transmitted to humans. Within days, dozens of people had also been infected. Most displayed only flulike symptoms, but in some cases, the illness escalated into a severe hemorrhagic fever akin to Ebola.

A similar scene was unfolding across the region. The survival rate in adult animals is as low as 10 percent, and nearly 100 percent of infected sheep abort their pregnancies. Dead lambs and calves were left bloating in fields until the state veterinary team came to collect and incinerate the carcasses. By the time the outbreak was under control, almost 9,000 animals and 25 people had died. Neighboring countries, such as Zimbabwe and Namibia, banned South African meat, shattering the livestock industry.

Ever since the virus was first identified in 1931 in Kenya's Rift Valley, outbreaks like this one had been confined to southern and eastern Africa. But in 1977 the disease migrated north through increased trade on the Nile River, causing what the World Health Organization called an "explosive outbreak" in Egypt. Then, in September of 2000, it jumped to the Arabian Peninsula, arriving in Saudi Arabia and Yemen–sparking anxiety that Europe and North America were next. The idea that the virus could spread across these continents in just a few years is not some hyperbolic scenario.

Rift is transmitted through a broader range of hosts and vectors than West Nile virus, which arrived in New York City in 1999 and spread across the U.S. in less than six years. The U.S. Department of Agriculture has taken notice, naming Rift the third most dangerous animal pathogen, behind only bird flu and foot-and-mouth disease. But health officials are not just worried about its impact on animals and agriculture. Zoonotic diseases–infectious illnesses such as Rift that begin in animal populations and jump to humans–are the biggest risk for epidemics and pandemics. They have been responsible for some of history's worst, including bubonic plague and Ebola.

The fear of Rift growing into a global pandemic highlights that public health researchers still don't know how to effectively predict disease outbreaks, which have devastating consequences on health, economies and political stability. Meanwhile the threat of emerging zoonotic diseases is expanding–and often in unforeseen ways. Scientists are only just beginning to understand how outbreaks correlate with shifting weather patterns–a hallmark of climate change. As they do, the picture is becoming more complicated. Worldwide, temperatures are changing faster than anyone previously predicted, and as a result, habitats are, too–altering the ranges of animals, viruses and, increasingly, humans. These complex relationships are now more volatile than ever, leading one recent *Lancet* paper to conclude that climate change is "the biggest global health threat in the 21st century" and yet another in the *Lancet* to suggest that it "threatens to undermine the last half century of gains in development and global health."

Global warming and extreme weather patterns are already dramatic forces on public health. Intensified floods, droughts and storms are changing how humans can use land and, ultimately, where we can live. As climatologists race to model what has changed so that coastal communities, for instance, can adapt to rising seas, epidemiologists are also realizing how critical it is to develop epidemic-prediction tools that incorporate new and impending weather patterns. Such research is a matter of equity between developing and developed nations. And in an ever more globalized world, it may be a way of averting a future of unprecedented pandemics.

An Interconnected Approach

To get to Steenkamp's farm, biologist Ettienne Theron has been driving for hours toward an endless horizon. His truck, loaded with coolers full of blood, bounces down a crumbling highway that is flanked by open grassland. These velds are where the last several Rift epidemics in South Africa began. It's here, in an area larger than the size of Maryland, that Theron and dozens more researchers are collecting and analyzing data for a project run by EcoHealth Alliance, a global nonprofit that focuses on pandemic prevention. [*Editor's Note: This story was reported before the COVID pandemic drew more attention to EcoHealth Alliance, which was a partner with the Wuhan Institute of Virology as part of its work around the world.*]

The challenge for scientists and policy makers alike is to learn how to intervene before pathogens infect people. Once a pandemic emerges, said EcoHealth president Peter Daszak in a 2015 video, "all you can really do is put out the fire." The goal of this five-year, multidisciplinary project is to examine, for the first time, exactly how climate affects Rift Valley fever in southern Africa. In doing so, researchers hope to develop a data-based model that actually predicts outbreaks before they happen, a stepping-stone to making models for other viruses as well. Notably, the U.S. Department of Defense has funded the entire project. Rift can easily be used as an aerosol and was weaponized by both the U.S. and the Soviet Union during the cold war. But bioterrorism is only one concern; keeping diseases from reaching the U.S.'s shores–and knowing how to react if they do–is increasingly a matter of national security.

Theron finally arrives at an unmarked gate, and the team members, who collectively speak nine of the languages represented in the Free State province, pile out of the truck and pull on muck boots. Using a random distribution of GPS points, the researchers have reached an agreement with 361 isolated farms like Steenkamp's, where, for two years in a row, they have taken blood samples from livestock and farm staff to test for Rift antibodies, trying to understand where the virus might be lurking when no one is reporting active cases.

Steenkamp himself was infected during an outbreak in the 1970s, and according to the WHO, as many as 10,000 people a year contract the virus. That number will most likely rise. A 2016 study published in *Emerging Microbes & Infections* reports that the "explosive nature" of recent epidemics suggests the virus has mutated into a more infectious and severe strain. As it migrates to new places, the virus may evolve further, becoming even more dangerous.

As the farm crew maneuvers sheep into a corner of a rusted corral, field coordinator Claudia Cordel unpacks an arrangement of empty vials, data sheets, latex gloves and a sharps box on a folding card table. A farm worker grabs an ewe. It bleats while Cordel draws blood from its jerking neck. In South Africa, *Aedes mcintoshi* mosquitoes are thought to be the main carrier of Rift. The females transmit the virus directly to offspring, and their eggs can survive years of drought–a typical occurrence in this region. When the new generation of infected mosquitoes eventually hatch, they transmit the virus to livestock and wildlife alike. The virus amplifies in these hosts, so that when wider-ranging mosquitoes, such as *Culex* and *Anopheles*, bite infected animals, the original outbreak transforms into a swift-moving epidemic.

In another corral, Cordel wipes a cow's anus before piercing its tail vein. The cow lows and lets loose a squirt of green liquid toward her face. Cordel explains that though the basics of the virus transmission are known, "we have no idea how wildlife impacts people or livestock, or vice versa," adding that the feedback cycles are completely undocumented. That is why the EcoHealth team wants to get a more granular look at the interactions of weather, plants, insects, animals and people. At 22 research sites around the Free State and Northern Cape provinces, researchers trapped mosquitoes to search for the virus, studying soil composition and vegetation and setting up mini weather stations to monitor local conditions in conjunction with satellite data. This kind of comprehensive approach, which required dozens of experts in epidemiology, ecology, climatology, veterinary medicine and entomology, is both costly and relatively rare. But it may be the future of understanding how infectious diseases emerge and spread.

"It makes sense that the health of an animal population is related to the health of the human population," says Melinda Rostal, one of the project's investigators. Animals often serve as early-warning signs of a new outbreak; in 2017 in Brazil, for example, local monkey populations were nearly wiped out eight months before a yellow fever epidemic. But structuring research around interactions among people, animals and the environment has only recently gained traction in the global health community. This strategy, first defined by epidemiologist Calvin Schwabe in 1964 and now called "One Health," is an increasingly popular intellectual framework for epidemiology. As far back as 400 B.C., Hippocrates understood that the environment–including weather–impacts disease, but systematically bringing together multidisciplinary research to better understand complex systems is relatively new. The U.S. Centers for Disease Control and Prevention did not establish a One Health office until 2009, when officials acknowledged that changing environmental interactions "have led to the emergence and reemergence of many diseases." Pursuing One Health research is expensive up front, but in the long run, it can actually be more efficient: by sending out collaborative teams instead of funding individual research trips, the EcoHealth Rift project reduced the cost of transportation for its study by 35 percent.

The longtime absence of this style of coordination is partly why the global health community is still playing catchup on emerging diseases. Consider Zika, for example: although it was first identified in Uganda in 1947, it was largely ignored until it began tearing through the Americas in 2015. Such diseases often lack attention when they first emerge because they affect the poorest populations of the world, meaning they are generally not profitable for pharmaceutical development. The result is that these so-called neglected tropical diseases, according to the CDC, have already cost 57 million years of life lost prematurely. So as one of the largest One Health projects to date, EcoHealth's Rift work is an important case study: Can broad, multidisciplinary research projects fill this dangerous knowledge gap?

As the setting sun turns the grass gold, Cordel and Theron finish the farm visit by checking on a weather station, where a lonely wind propeller ticks above barbed wire. Satellite data from NASA suggest that this region will see altered weather patterns, changing its risk of both Rift and other infectious diseases. Transmission is a complicated thing, but undoubtedly a key factor in future disease control will be understanding the implications of our changing climate.

Forecasting Climate on a Backyard Scale

On the long drives between field sites, dead sunflowers droop under a relentless sky. South Africa has been in a drought for a few years, and the red soil has frazzled into puzzle pieces. Drought itself is a standard feature of El Niño weather patterns, and when La Niña eventually comes and completes the cycle, the area will see heavy rains. But these cycles, while typical, are intensifying because of climate change, becoming drier and wetter, explains Assaf Anyamba, a research scientist at the NASA Goddard Space Flight Center. (In March 2018 South Africa declared a "national state of disaster" over its prolonged drought. Cape Town was at risk of running out of water during the worst drought in 400 years.) Even as conditions grow more extreme, Anyamba says, the downpour associated with this rain pattern–known as the El Niño/Southern Oscillation (ENSO)–and the vegetable life that downpour creates are what makes it possible to predict the hatching of Rift-infected mosquitoes. In fact, Anyamba was able to successfully predict the 2006 and 2007 Rift outbreak in East Africa by adding satellite climate models to the mix instead of just relying on regional weather patterns. "To my knowledge," he says, "this is the only system of its kind for any disease."

With that promising model in hand, Anyamba looked to southern Africa and the Arabian Peninsula. If he could apply the tools he used in eastern Africa to predict Rift outbreaks elsewhere, perhaps he could expand the model to other diseases. But so far his Rift models have failed in South Africa. As the climate expert on the EcoHealth study, Anyamba is now trying to figure out why. Satellite data that show and forecast global weather patterns make it easier to predict changes with vegetation and insects. The downside is that this big-picture view is fairly imprecise. When researchers combine climate models with more granular regional data such as vegetation coverage, they are dealing with two different scales. Anyamba's eastern African satellite models relied on a vegetation index, for example, that did not reflect southern African plant species. Other factors that impact disease, such as the spread of vectors, can be even finer-grained. Many mosquitoes live in an area the size of a suburban backyard, so even remotely sensed data do not get at the scale with which pathogens interact with their hosts. Although weather has long been linked with disease–think "flu season"–it is this level of specificity that makes predicting outbreaks so challenging. A one-size-fits-all template will not work.

Anyamba's new tactic is to use the information the EcoHealth team gathers on mosquitoes and vegetation in South Africa to build a more customized prediction model for the region. Climate change may eventually make the Free State province drier, which would help prevent Rift outbreaks. Other parts of the country, however, will likely get warmer and wetter, increasing Rift and the other diseases that floods tend to foster. Learning how to build more regionally sensitive tools will help scientists understand how disease burdens may change, both locally and globally.

Getting there is a matter of urgency. While it is rare to find sweeping conclusions in epidemiology, it is clear that greater climate variability–and therefore greater disease fluctuation–is already here. The first conclusive evidence of the trend was likely initially reported in a 2002 study published in the *Proceedings of the National Academy of Sciences USA*, which looked at cholera prevalence in

Bangladesh over a 70-year period and found that "warming trends over the last century are affecting human disease." Mosquito and other insect habitats have expanded because of warming, exposing new populations to viruses. Preliminary research shows that malaria, for example, is globally on the rise. A temperature bump of just two degrees Celsius—a mark we are quickly approaching—would expand the number of people at risk of malaria by several hundred million, according to the WHO. Strangely, places that are now ideal climates for malaria may see less of it as they warm; prevalence will likely occur where malaria has not yet arrived, such as the U.S.

This type of vexing nuance has troubling consequences. Take bluetongue virus, a highly lethal ruminant disease that is spread by biting midges called *Culicoides*. Historically it was confined to tropical regions, but by 2006 there was enough warming in western Europe that some of those midges moved north and infected animals. Scientists were surprised when another kind of midge then picked up the virus from sickened sheep and carried it all the way to Norway. Corrie Brown, a veterinary pathologist at the University of Georgia, says bluetongue is a prime example of how climate change introduces species to one another for the first time—expanding how diseases can spread in an unpredictable manner.

Experts disagree on the best way to handle these risks. The U.S. Agency for International Development supports a strategy that focuses on identifying new pathogens, but Brown thinks merely discovering new viruses is an inefficient use of limited research funding. "I can see how very good it'd be for the investigators because they'd get a lot of papers published," Brown says, but she is bearish on its value in preventing people from getting sick. Instead Brown and others who advocate for a One Health approach think strengthening local infrastructure—building monitoring and surveillance systems and training community nurses, for instance—is the most effective way to grapple with the fickle burdens of emerging diseases. "If we improve the level of expertise of health-care professionals all around the world, we'll be in a better place," she says.

Local detection systems are especially important in places where humans are the ones who have moved into new environments, exposing themselves to diseases they have not yet encountered. "In an unchanging world, you don't see a lot of emerging disease," says William Karesh, an epidemiologist and the Rift study's principal investigator. "It's when systems alter that microbes reveal themselves in new ways." Often epidemics and their ripple effects "happen at the edge, where humans are living next to wild spaces," says Carrie La Jeunesse, a former AAAS Congressional Science & Technology Policy Fellow who worked on Ebola. Since 2009 USAID has developed a heat map for emerging diseases with pandemic potential; it is remarkably similar to maps of regions threatened by human impact. In a 2012 paper published in the *Lancet*, Karesh and his colleagues summarized these findings by explaining that "many zoonoses can be linked to large-scale changes in land use."

That is certainly true in South Africa. "We actually farm with arboviruses," the viruses transmitted by arthropods such as ticks, says Alan Kemp, an entomologist on the EcoHealth project. "With Rift, it's almost certain that thanks to cattle breeding and importing exotic breeds that aren't resistant, we're actually literally farming Rift." He sighs and says, "To be honest, to a large extent, we're guilty of our own demise."

The Human Strain

The thousands of blood samples EcoHealth has procured end up under the fluorescent gleam of a biosafety level–four laboratory in Johannesburg. Like Ebola, work with Rift is allowed only in the highest level of containment, and investigator Janusz Paweska wears a pressurized protective suit to examine Rift specimens under a microscope. "Some scientists refer to nature as the most terrible bioterrorist, which I dislike," says Paweska from his office, after he has been through the elaborate decontamination process. As head of South Africa's Center for Emerging Zoonotic and Parasitic Diseases, he does not mince words: "Who creates this environment for emergence? You can't accuse nature. Uncontrolled urbanization, climate change, poverty–that's not nature. The answer is that we create the situation for the emergence of many of these diseases."

Arguably poverty is already the greatest risk factor for getting sick. "The major trigger or determinant of health is economic," says Antoine Flahault, director of the Institute of Global Health in Geneva, explaining that an unequal distribution of health care is the primary problem. The WHO estimates that in low-income countries, diseases of poverty that are often preventable or treatable (think diarrhea, malnutrition and parasitic infections) account for 45 percent of deaths. Climate change is expected to drive at least 122 million people into extreme poverty in the next few decades, forcing many to leave their homes and leading to rapid urbanization, all of which tends to foster disease. Flahault expects that one of the major disease contributions of climate change will come from these consequences of forced migration. "We can expect a huge impact on health, not just because of direct impact on disease but because of the indirect economic impacts, which may be very severe," Flahault says.

But when countries with limited resources are asked to prepare for a future potential threat, often at the cost of immediate problems, "it's a hard trade-off," explains Susan Scribner, director of the Preparedness & Response project at the global development firm DAI. "What we do is called health, but in some ways, a lot of it has to do with good governance," she says. That is why projects such as the Rift study could be particularly powerful: they provide data to many different stakeholders spanning agriculture, health and defense.

Anyamba, EcoHealth's climate expert, sees the Rift study as the way of the future. "I envision more projects involving climate data, fused with advanced analytics and machine-learning technologies, that will begin to answer some questions [about] why particular disease outbreaks occur," he says. Policy makers may be juggling other priorities, but it is important that they understand this science, Scribner says, "because when a pandemic hits, scientists aren't the ones in charge of the response." In fact, the DOD's Defense Threat Reduction Agency funded similarly comprehensive research to predict and map areas at risk for chikungunya, another mosquito-borne viral infection. There is a long list of diseases, such as yellow fever, dengue and even rabies, that would benefit from the kind of resources the DOD can bring to bear.

But funding–and the politics that go into deciding whose research gets it–plays a critical role in which diseases are deemed worthy of attention. In the current political climate, support for the long-term resources that logistically complex projects (such as the Rift study) require is actively disappearing. Just as we are beginning to realize how urgent a collaborative approach to disease might be, the CDC has faced massive threats to its global health security efforts. Funding global health is a complex endeavor managed by multiple agencies in the U.S. alone. Experts at the Brookings Institution think tank have written that it could be "devastating for global health," damaging economic growth as well as weakening international stability.

But the importance of doing this kind of intensive fieldwork continues. Amid this limbo, EcoHealth's sweeping fieldwork presses on. Early one morning during its collection process, the team pulls up to a private game reserve near Mokala National Park to chase down kudu, a type of African antelope. Wildlife can both carry and transmit Rift to livestock and humans, but their blood samples are especially tricky to obtain. A helicopter arrives to lend a hand. Soon trucks are bouncing over the grass, a cloud of dust marking progress toward the herd. Beyond the front tires, the animals swerve and leap. They gleam like ribbons. The stillness when one is tranquilized from the sky is shocking. The scientists work quickly, sliding around a maze of arms and legs with syringes and vials. The kudu will wake in a matter of minutes.

After the blood is collected, the researchers begin their decontamination procedures, scrubbing dust off their boots to avoid spreading any diseases to the next property they visit. Nearby, a caged lion lounges in a puddle of sunshine, awaiting the delivery of his next meal. He yawns at the stream of passing cars. Once this bushveld stretched wild over half of the country, but today it has been largely partitioned off and contained behind tall fences. There are few places now where wildlife are still able to wander free. The world has already changed, even if we do not yet know the consequences.

Referenced

Tackling Climate Change: The Greatest Opportunity for Global Health. Helena Wang and Richard Horton in *Lancet*, Vol. 386, pages 1798–1799; November 7, 2015.

Rift Valley Fever: An Emerging Mosquito-Borne Disease. Kenneth J. Linthicum et al. in *Annual Review of Entomology*, Vol. 61, pages 395–415; 2016.

Global Hotspots and Correlates of Emerging Zoonotic Diseases. Toph Allen et al. in *Nature Communications*, Vol. 8, Article No. 1124; October 24, 2017.

About the Author

Lois Parshley is an award-winning freelance journalist whose work has appeared in Harper's Magazine, the Atlantic, Wired *and many other publications. She was a 2017–2018 Knight-Wallace journalism fellow and is a former editor at* Popular Science *and* Foreign Policy*.*

Climate Change Hastened Syria's Civil War

By Mark Fischetti

Climate change can make storms stronger, cold spells longer and water supplies drier. But can it cause war? A new study published today in *Proceedings of the National Academy of Sciences* says drought in Syria, exacerbated to record levels by global warming, pushed social unrest in that nation across a line into an open uprising in 2011. The conflict has since become a major civil war with international involvement.

Drying and drought in Syria from 2006 to 2011—the worst on record there—destroyed agriculture, causing many farm families to migrate to cities. The influx added to social stresses already created by refugees pouring in from the war in Iraq, explains Richard Seager, a climate scientist at Columbia University's Lamont-Doherty Earth Observatory who co-authored the study. The drought also pushed up food prices, aggravating poverty. "We're not saying the drought caused the war," Seager said. "We're saying that added to all the other stressors, it helped kick things over the threshold into open conflict. And a drought of that severity was made much more likely by the ongoing human-driven drying of that region."

Seager added that the entire Middle East "faces a drier, hotter climate due to climate change. This will stress water resources and agriculture, and will likely further increase risk of conflict." Global warming is desiccating the region in two ways: higher temperatures that increase evaporation in already parched soils, and weaker winds that bring less rain from the Mediterranean Sea during the wet season (November to April).

A number of research efforts in recent years have suggested that warmer temperatures and drought increase the risk of violent conflict around the world. A 2009 study found that over the past 30 years in sub-Saharan Africa, temperature rise correlated with an increase in the likelihood of civil war. A 2011 study implicated climate change in pushing up food prices in Egypt, fueling revolution there.

Trouble related to drought in the Middle East may get worse. The United Nations Intergovernmental Panel on Climate Change has predicted that human effects on climate change will make the area drier than it would have become without the manmade influences.

The U.S. Defense Department is taking the warning seriously. It issued a report last November declaring climate change a "threat multiplier" that will impact national security. When *Scientific American* asked Seager if his group's research supports that point of view he said, "Yes. It does. Climate change is very much a cause of concern for national, regional and international security and this study makes clear how that can work. The Syrian war has now taken on a life of its own...however, a drought made worse by climate change was one important factor that initiated the social unraveling."

Colin Kelley, a climatologist at the University of California, Santa Barbara, who led the work while finishing his doctorate at Lamont-Doherty, concurred, but was also careful to state that severe droughts can have a catalytic effect and contribute to, but not cause, civil unrest.

Although snowstorms and rising sea levels garner more of the headlines about extreme weather driven by climate change, drought is quickly rising as the most troublesome, near-term impact. Another paper in PNAS suggests links between global warming and the terrible, ongoing drought in California. Although civil unrest is far less likely there, tension is indeed growing between political leaders in northern and southern California over who gets the increasingly scarce water from rivers, underground aquifers and snow melt, all of which are declining.

About the Author

Mark Fischetti is a senior editor at Scientific American. He covers all aspects of sustainability. Follow him on Twitter @markfischetti

Climate Change Is Creating New Vocabulary, from Eco-Anxiety to Kaitiakitanga

By Trish Stewart

Climate change is everywhere in the news this week, as nations attending the 26th United Nations Climate Change Conference of the Parties (COP26) firm their commitments to reduce carbon dioxide emissions. But did you know that the language of climate change and sustainability–from "eco-anxiety" to "climate crisis"–is constantly evolving to reflect new realities and concerns? Some terms have surged, others have taken on a revised meaning, and some are just brand new. In response to these rapid changes in vocabulary, I and my colleagues at the *Oxford English Dictionary* (*OED*) have just finished reviewing the dictionary's coverage of language related to climate change and sustainability, revising and updating entries already in the dictionary and adding new ones. Some words have a much longer history than might be expected, and some reveal more general shifts in language usage.

"Climate change" remains the most commonly employed term to describe the effects of increasing levels of CO_2 in the atmosphere. Related terms such as "global warming" and "greenhouse effect" have decreased in use. There has been a deliberate shift by some news organizations to use stronger and more emotive language, however. As a result, "climate crisis" and "climate emergency" are increasingly used to communicate a sense of urgency about the problem. In some cases, "climate" itself is used as shorthand for "climate change": a "climate skeptic," or "climate denier," is someone who doubts that climate change exists or that human activity contributes to it.

The earliest example of "climate change" we found was from an 1854 article about milder winters occurring in Europe. That early usage shows that, even then, there was disagreement over whether human activity such as draining marshes and clearing forests could cause changes in climate or whether the changes were linked to some other cause–in this case the changeable position of the Earth's magnetic poles. People forced to flee the effects of climate change are "climate refugees," but that term was first used in American newspapers at the end of the 19th century to refer to residents who moved to a place where the climate was more congenial or beneficial. California was the location of choice in the earliest examples we found.

The *OED* does not generally include chemical formulas, but we have added "CO_2" as an exception. It joins "NOX" and "H2O" as the only examples in the dictionary. The use of CO_2 rather than "carbon dioxide" in the context of environmental issues and climate change is now so ingrained in our language that it warrants its own *OED* entry. The formula has come to function as a word.

New technologies developed to reduce our reliance on fossil fuels can also lead to new terminology. A move to the smart charging of electric vehicles has resulted in the appearance of "range anxiety," the worry that car batteries may not take drivers as far as they wish. Sometimes, though, what appears to be recent technology may not be not so new after all. We've added a new definition of "windmill" that means a wind turbine that generates electricity. But the potential for windmills to be used in this way was recognized as far back as 1879. Later in the 19th century, a Norwegian Arctic exploration ship was even fitted with a windmill to supply electricity for lighting onboard. The appearance of this new terminology is heartening and demonstrates the variety of solutions to climate change that are becoming available.

The rise of eco-anxiety–the unease or apprehension about current and future harm to the environment, in this case caused by climate change and its effects–is sobering. But there is also increasing recognition of our impact on the environment and a growing impetus for change. The addition of the Māori loanword "kaitiakitanga," the human duty or responsibility of environmental stewardship, reminds us that we all have a part to play in creating a sustainable future.

About the Author

Trish Stewart is a senior science editor at the Oxford English Dictionary. *Her work focuses on updating and increasing the dictionary's coverage of words related to biology and the life sciences.*

How Cities Can Protect Themselves from Rising Waters

By Ziqian (Cecilia) Dong

Across the U.S., policymakers are scrambling to protect their communities from the effects of climate change.

In January, Massachusetts Governor Charlie Baker proposed real-estate tax increases to fund dam and drainage system upgrades, which would help residents cope with future floods and storms. Meanwhile, a few months earlier, officials from several Florida counties agreed to work together to minimize the damage caused by rising sea levels.

Adaptation efforts like these are crucial. Four in 10 Americans live in coastal areas. and this population will surge in the coming years. Sustained flooding can cripple homes and infrastructure like roads, bridges, subways and wastewater treatment plants.

Policymakers have limited time and resources, so they should rely on the latest computer modeling and other technologies to identify and implement the most efficient adaptation strategies.

Rising water levels have already wrought havoc across the country. From 2000 to 2015, coastal "sunny day flooding," or flooding caused by high tides rather than storms, more than doubled on the Southeast's Atlantic coast, according to the National Oceanic and Atmospheric Association. And it increased 75 percent on the Northeast's coast.

Climate change is also making storms more destructive and frequent by heating up ocean waters, increasing flooding. The United States experienced its most expensive hurricane season in history in 2017; storms caused more than $300 billion in damages. Flooding and other damage from Hurricane Harvey alone forced 37,000 Texans into shelters in September 2017. Last year, Hurricane Michael caused at least 45 deaths and more than $12 billion in losses.

Worse still, our country is losing natural defenses against flooding. Between 2004 and 2009, 80,000 acres of U.S. coastal wetlands–which soak up flood waters–disappeared each year, largely as a consequence of development. Mangrove forests–which help block sea waters–are also declining, thanks to human activity. Mangrove acreage at Lake Worth near West Palm Beach, for example, has plummeted 87 percent within the past four decades, according to government data.

Floods and storms will grow more intense in the coming decades. Computer modeling and visualization tools can help us identify the weakest links and plan strategically.

Consider work by researchers at Texas A&M University. They conducted a simulation of Southeast Florida that demonstrated how rising seas will damage the road network. It found that installing water pumps now would save money in the long run. Another analysis showed the effects of saltwater intrusion on water wells and identified which wells were in need of upgrades.

Or take IN-SOURCE, a 3-D modeling framework and visualization tool that my team at New York Institute of Technology, along with partners in the U.S., Germany and Austria, is developing. This visualization tool will enable utility companies and government officials to identify areas that are most vulnerable to extreme weather events and assess the effectiveness of potential infrastructure improvements.

Various emerging technologies can help communities get the most out of their investments. For one, microgrids: the tiny electric grids that can supply a single building or neighborhood with electricity, usually generated from renewable energy sources. These distributed power sources can operate independently and don't rely on miles of power lines, so they're less vulnerable to extreme weather events.

Putting critical food or water distribution centers on their own microgrids could help people and their cities be more resilient to future superstorms. The Hunts Point food-distribution center in Bronx, New York, for example, which provides 60 percent of metro

New York's produce, meat and fish, is located in a flood zone. With a microgrid, this center could keep running even if power lines go down.

Spending money up-front to evaluate adaptation initiatives saves money in the long run. Consider one project in St. Paul, Minnesota. Storm water runoff caused frequent local flooding in the Capitol Region Watershed District. Officials evaluated several plans and decided on a strategy that utilized green infrastructure and special techniques like rain gardens–in which shrubs and plants capture rain water. Thanks to these improvements, flooding decreased dramatically. And the plan was found to be cost-effective.

Meanwhile, in Portland, Oregon–which was ravaged by a monstrous flood in 1996–officials have taken many steps to improve flood management using green infrastructure. They reported that putting just $9 million into such initiatives saved $224 million in sewer overflow costs–so far.

Communities–both in the U.S. and worldwide–must prepare now for severe storms and rising seas. New technology can help them invest their resources wisely. And with the right infrastructure upgrades, communities can minimize future damages and save lives.

This was originally published as an opinion piece. The views expressed are those of the author(s) and are not necessarily those of Scientific American.

About the Author

Ziqian (Cecilia) Dong, PhD, is an associate professor in the Department of Electrical and Computer Engineering at New York Institute of Technology.

Section 4: The Policy and Politics of Climate Change

Three Things We Must Do to Tackle Climate Change

By Susan Joy Hassol, Jerry Melillo

With world leaders meeting at the international climate change conference in Glasgow to negotiate urgent global action necessary to meet this greatest of challenges, many people still don't know what must be done. Ever since the "code red" report from the Intergovernmental Panel on Climate Change (IPCC) this August, many people have been feeling shell-shocked. In addition to bringing a serious dose of reality to those who don't keep up with the latest advances in climate science, the most important message of the report is that it is not too late to avoid the worst impacts of climate change, if we act rapidly and decisively to cut the emissions that are warming our planet. But what would that look like?

It comes down to three things: phase out fossil fuels, deploy clean energy, and protect the world's forests.

To phase out fossil fuels, the first step is to allow no new development of coal, oil and gas. That means no exploration, no new wells, mines, pipelines, refineries or power plants. We already have a massive amount of fossil fuel infrastructure, and it will take decades to phase out its use. It makes no sense to throw good money after bad and prolong the inevitable. The International Energy Agency has concluded that any new fossil fuel investments from now on would be incompatible with meeting internationally agreed-upon climate targets.

After a phaseout of existing internal combustion engine vehicles, all new cars, trucks, buses, and trains should be electric or powered by other clean fuels such as green hydrogen. It will be years before all the dirty old vehicles are off the road, but good policies can help speed that transition.

Another important aspect of the fossil fuel phaseout is to plug methane leaks associated with current and former coal, oil and gas development. The IPCC report makes clear that reducing these emissions is the best opportunity to avoid a significant amount of near-term warming.

Methane is a potent heat-trapping gas, about 80 times as powerful as carbon dioxide over a 20-year period. It also has a much shorter atmospheric lifetime than carbon dioxide, so its levels can be reduced relatively quickly. Oil and gas wells and pipelines and coal mines often leak large amounts of methane. Plugging these leaks will save money, improve air quality, and stave off warming. We now have the technologies to find and eliminate these leaks.

Second of our three major tasks is rapidly ramping up the deployment of clean, renewable energy. Contrary to a common misconception, we do not need an energy miracle, because we've already had one. Solar and wind are the fastest-growing new sources of energy we have. Their costs have plummeted, making them the least expensive options in most locations. Studies have shown that we can get all the power we need from wind, water and sun coupled with various kinds of energy storage and grid improvements.

Part of clean energy deployment involves recognizing the global nature of the climate challenge and developing aggressive and efficient ways to share clean energy technologies across the globe. Many people in developing countries do not yet have access to reliable electricity. It is a global imperative to help them gain this access through new, clean technologies. Just as countries that lacked telephone service were able to leapfrog over conventional phone lines and go straight to mobile phones, they can similarly skip the dirty energy stage and go straight to renewable energy.

Third of our tasks is protecting the world's forests, which currently absorb about a third of the carbon dioxide our activities emit to the atmosphere. Tropical forests are especially at risk and still being cleared for agricultural uses including cattle ranching and soybean and palm oil production, and this must cease. To meet the planet's growing food needs, agronomists urge improved management practices on already-cleared land rather than clearing new land, especially forested land. We must recognize that maintaining these vital carbon sinks is of value to all life on Earth, and we must be willing to do whatever it takes to help protect them.

All three of these tasks will serve us in many ways beyond ensuring a livable climate. Protecting forests will not only maintain their vital function as a carbon sink, it will also help preserve indigenous cultures, biological diversity, endangered species and clean air and water.

Similarly, ending new fossil fuel development and phasing out its existing uses will give us cleaner air and water, better health, fewer premature deaths and less of the toxic pollution that comes with oil spills, mountaintop removal and other insults that accompany the extraction and use of fossil fuels.

Finally, the global cooperation could be transformative for humanity as we work together to protect the only home we have. If we can see beyond our typical battle lines, we can take on this global challenge as we would if some outside force were inflicting it upon us. We are on a mission to save planet Earth, its people and its natural wonders. The three actions we propose–phasing out fossil fuels, deploying clean energy and protecting the world's forests–are essential for success.

About the Authors

Susan Joy Hassol is the director of Climate Communication and recipient of the 2021 Ambassador Award of the American Geophysical Union.

Jerry Melillo is a Distinguished Scientist at the Marine Biological Laboratory and a member of the National Academy of Sciences.

Climate Deniers Shift Tactics to 'Inactivism'

By Richard Schiffman

Michael Mann is no stranger to the war against climate science. A climatologist at Pennsylvania State University who is currently studying the impact of climate change on extreme weather events, Mann is best known for the "hockey stick graph," which he and his colleagues published in a 1998 scientific paper. The data visualization—featured prominently in former vice president Al Gore's documentary An Inconvenient Truth—illustrates the precipitous rise in global temperatures since the dawn of the industrial era.

The graph also helped make the researcher a target of attacks by climate change deniers. Mann's e-mails were stolen, and he was investigated by government bodies and received death threats in a years-long campaign he says was orchestrated by fossil fuel companies and their allies to discredit his work. Those experiences compelled him to "enter the fray" and "speak out about the very real implications of our research," he wrote in an op-ed in the New York Times in 2014.

Although it is too soon to declare victory, Mann cautions, the initial war of disinformation against climate science is now essentially over. The scientific evidence has become impossible to dispute in light of the dramatic increases in extreme weather events, megafires and polar melting in recent years, he says.

The deniers have not given up the battle, however. They have merely changed their tactics, Mann contends in his book The New Climate War: The Fight to Take Back Our Planet. He spoke with *Scientific American* about the book and why he believes that the world is finally getting ready to move more aggressively on the climate crisis.

[*An edited transcript of the interview follows.*]

Q: You argue that the climate change deniers are going extinct and being replaced by a new group that you call "the inactivists." Who are the inactivists?

A: The plutocrats who are tied to the fossil fuel industry are engaging in a new climate war–this time to prevent meaningful action. Over the past few years, you've seen a lot of conservative groups pulling their money out of the climate-change-denial industry and putting it instead into efforts by ALEC [the American Legislative Exchange Council, a conservative lobbying group], for example, to fund legislative efforts blocking clean-energy policies.

Q: The book details the way these fossil fuel interests are working to dampen the public's enthusiasm for taking action on climate. How are they doing that?

A: I use whole bunch of "D" words to describe this: deflection, delay, division, despair mongering, doomism. To start with, there is an effort to deflect attention away from systemic solutions. They are trying to convince people that climate change is not the result of their corporate policies but of our own individual actions. I mean BP [a multinational oil and gas company headquartered in London] was instrumental in the whole idea of a carbon footprint. They introduced the carbon footprint calculator to help get people to think of this as an individual-responsibility issue.

Q: You mean if people believe that their lifestyle choices are to blame for climate change, they won't pressure big energy companies to cut their production of fossil fuels or support the development of cleaner alternatives?

A: That's the idea. One of the best examples of this sort of deflection campaign is the gun lobby's motto "Guns don't kill people, people do."

Q: So that concept has morphed into "Fossil fuels don't cause climate change, people do"?

A: Exactly. If you can get people arguing over these individual lifestyle choices, then you are creating division over questions such as "Are you vegan or not?" "Do you fly?" So it's a twofer–you deflect attention away from the need for real policy change, and you get infighting within the climate movement so that climate advocates are not speaking with one coherent voice.

Q: You're not suggesting that people shouldn't change their behavior, are you?

A: We should definitely try to be the best stewards of the planet that we can be. It saves us money, makes us healthier and sets a good example for others. But let's not allow that to be used as a crutch for the failure to demand larger policy interventions to tackle this problem. Voluntary efforts alone are not going to achieve the kind of reductions we need. We need powerful financial incentives–policies such as subsidies for renewables and effective carbon pricing schemes.

Q: One of your "D" words is division. Can you give some concrete examples of how the fossil fuel industry has been working to create divisions within the environmental community?

A: An e-mail sent to journalists in 2020 by CRC Advisors [a PR firm that represents industry players and others] contained talking points that appeared to attempt to sow racial division within the climate movement. The e-mail suggested that the Green New Deal–supported by white environmentalists–would hurt minority communities. It is an attempt to drive a wedge right down the center of the progressive movement–between social activists and climate activists.

Another case involves Michael Moore's recent documentary Planet of the Humans, which contains a laundry list of deceptive facts and bad arguments against renewable energy. An industry advocacy group known as the American Energy Alliance spent thousands of dollars promoting this film. Conservative foundations and media outlets all came out of the woodwork to support the film.

Q: You say that fossil fuel interests are not just fighting against renewable energy. They are also pushing the idea that it is too late—that climate change cannot be stopped, and it is pointless to try to do so at this stage.

A: Conservative media are promoting people such as Guy McPherson, who says that we have 10 years left before exponential climate change literally extinguishes life on Earth and that we should somehow find a way to cope with our imminent demise. I call it "climate doom porn." It's very popular, it really sells magazines, but it's incredibly disabling. If you believe that we have no agency, then why take any action? I'm not saying that fossil fuel companies are funding people like McPherson; I have no evidence of that. But when you look at who is actually pushing this message, it's the conservative media networks that air his interviews.

Q: Some of your scientist colleagues criticize you for asserting that there is a "war" being waged against climate policy. How do you respond?

A: I respond that the easiest way to lose a war is to deny that you are in one. This is not a war that we choose to be in. But powerful interests have engineered the most well-funded and elaborate public relations campaign in the history of Earth to block progress on climate. We need to recognize that these are not actors who are going to play nice with us. They are not engaged in a good faith conversation based on facts and logical arguments.

Q: After detailing the systematic efforts to block action on climate in the book, you say that you are optimistic. What makes you hopeful?

A: We're not going to get a Green New Deal, not from this Congress. But we might get a climate bill that involves market mechanisms, as well as incentives. President-elect Joe Biden is pretty pragmatic on this. He's appointed John Kerry [as special presidential envoy for climate], who is capable of pulling that off. I think we're headed toward some kind of market approach to dealing with climate.

Q: You write that young activists inspire you. How so?

A: I don't always quote the Bible, but when I do, I say, "And a child shall lead them." The young have really moved the needle. For too long, we have allowed this issue to be framed entirely as one of science or economics or policy and politics. But more than anything else, it's about ethics, our obligation not to destroy this planet for future generations. People of good will are finally demanding action. I think it's because our children have come out and demanded it of the adults of the world.

About the Author

Richard Schiffman is an environmental journalist based in New York City.

To Understand How Science Denial Works, Look to History

By Naomi Oreskes

2020 has been a historic year– and mostly not in a good way. Among many things, we saw a historic level of disregard of scientific advice with respect to the COVID-19 virus, a disregard that made the pandemic worse in the U.S. than in many other countries. But while the events of 2020 may feel unprecedented, the social pattern of rejecting scientific evidence did not suddenly appear this year. There was never any good scientific reason for rejecting the expert advice on COVID, just as there has never been any good scientific reason for doubting that humans evolved, that vaccines save lives, and that greenhouse gases are driving disruptive climate change. To understand the social pattern of rejecting scientific findings and expert advice, we need to look beyond science to history, which tells us that many of the various forms of the rejection of expert evidence and the promotion of disinformation have roots in the history of tobacco.

Throughout the first half of the 20th century, most Americans saw science as something that made our lives better. Science had deepened our understanding of the natural world, which helped us to cure diseases, light our homes and bring new forms of entertainment into our lives. Perhaps most important, physicists helped to win World War II and became cultural heroes. Chemists got their due, too. As DuPont reminded us, we had "better things for better living through chemistry." At General Electric, scientists and engineers were helping to "bring good things to life." These were not just slogans; corporate R&D really did produce products that measurably improved many American lives. But corporate America was also developing the playbook for science denial and disinformation.

The chief culprit in this darker story was the tobacco industry, whose playbook has been well documented by historians of science, technology and medicine, as well as epidemiologists and lawyers. It disparaged science by promoting the idea that the link between tobacco use and lung cancer and other diseases was uncertain or incomplete and that the attempt to regulate it was a threat to American freedom. The industry made products more addictive by increasing their nicotine content while publicly denying that nicotine was addictive. With these tactics, the industry was able to delay effective measures to discourage smoking long after the scientific evidence of its harms was clear. In our 2010 book, *Merchants of Doubt*, Erik M. Conway and I showed how the same arguments were used to delay action on acid rain, the ozone hole and climate change–and this year we saw the spurious "freedom" argument being used to disparage mask wearing.

We also saw the tobacco strategy seeping into social media, which influences public opinion and which many people feel needs to be subject to greater scrutiny and perhaps government regulation. In October 2019, Congress held hearings to investigate the role of Facebook in potentially spreading misinformation. In the summer of 2020 a report from civil-rights law firm Relman Colfax suggested that Facebook posts could contribute to voter suppression. Climate scientists have complained that the social media giant contributes to the spread of climate denial by permitting false or misleading claims while hobbling responses by mainstream scientists by labeling their posts "political."

Without a historical perspective, we might interpret this as a novel problem created by a novel technology. But this past September, a former Facebook manager testified in Congress that the company "took a page from Big Tobacco's playbook, working to make our offering addictive," saying that Facebook was determined to make people addicted to its products while publicly using the euphemism of increasing "engagement." Like the tobacco industry, social media companies sold us a toxic product while insisting that it was simply giving consumers what they wanted.

Scientific colleagues often ask me why I traded a career in science for a career in history. History, for some of them, is just "dwelling on the past." But, as the bard said in *The Tempest*: "What's past is prologue." If we are to confront disinformation, the rejection of scientific findings, and the negative uses of technology, we have to understand the past that has brought us to this point."

About the Author

Naomi Oreskes is a professor of the history of science at Harvard University. She is author of Why Trust Science? *(Princeton University Press, 2019) and co-author of* Discerning Experts *(University of Chicago, 2019).*

Our Environmental Crisis Requires Political Fixes, Not Technological Ones

By Peter Sutoris

Whether via West Coast wildfires that shrouded New York City's skyline in smoke or historic floods in Germany, in 2021, signs of the climate crisis were everywhere. A group of the world's leading ecologists summarized humanity's predicament when they recently argued that our main goal now as a species is to "avoid a ghastly future."

So far, we have responded to the threat of environmental collapse primarily by trying to modify our technologies, whether in moving away from combustion engines or making solar energy cheaper and more efficient. Many policymakers, scientists, and opinion leaders believe that we are moving in the right direction. Their main concern is whether we'll move fast enough to avoid the greatest environmental catastrophes.

These ideas might sound out of touch with reality. And this is exactly my point: our inability to conceptualize bold changes signals a crisis of political imagination that's at the root of what political scientist Karen Litfin calls the "mounting socioecological multicrisis."

And I deliberately refer to the term *multicrisis* rather than *climate change* because what we're witnessing is a multitude of interconnected crises. The public conversation revolves around cutting down emissions in order to slow down global warming, but the harsh truth is that even if we had a magic button that could stop all emissions overnight, even if we could remain within 1.5 degrees of warming (now an unlikely outcome), we'd still be left with multiple other existential crises. We remain wedded to ideologies that have caused this mess in the first place, such as extractivism, the belief that the Earth is ours to exploit, and speciesism, the idea that humans are superior to all other species.

Biodiversity loss and ecosystem collapse are caused by myriad reasons other than climate change, from chemical pollutants released into the environment to the damming of rivers to invasive species transported around the world through global trade and travel. Each threatened species' predicament is different, and there is no single tech solution that can solve this crisis. Plus there's the crisis of the phosphate and nitrogen cycles, overdrafting of water reservoirs, overfishing, deforestation–the list goes on and on.

Once we grasp this complexity, it becomes evident that we need to reimagine our society and our future. Recognizing that climate change is simply just one facet of a larger multicrisis might feel paralyzing or even hopeless; but it is, in fact, freeing. It helps us realize that some of our current paradigms are simply not fit for sustainability, and that it's time to get truly creative.

Political imagination is powerful because it can turn seemingly radical ideas into attainable objectives. We've seen this repeatedly in history: grassroots resistance of political activists helped wear down the apartheid regime in South Africa. In the 1960s and 1970s, Cold War dissidents first imagined democracy in Eastern Europe in clandestine writings, called samizdats, before their societies started seeing it as a realistic possibility. History teaches us that the path to deep change is paved with radical imagination. It also teaches us that while change can happen faster than we might expect, it rarely happens overnight, which is why we need to start now.

What might political imagination allow us to do differently today? Instead of an economy driven by the diktat of infinite growth, we might steer our trajectory in the direction of stable-state economies, even as we preserve markets and healthy competition between businesses. We might pass legislation that recognizes the rights of future generations and the rights of other species to autonomy, allowing the judiciary to uphold a much higher standard of environmental protection than what's possible under current frameworks.

Last summer, a landmark study suggested we might be seeing early signs of the Gulf Stream's collapse, and the IPCC released its most pointed warning yet about the gravity of climate change. The urgency could hardly be greater. Embracing radical political imagination as the path forward would have a dramatic impact on how our civilization relates to the natural world and to the future, which would in turn bring us closer to solving the multicrisis.

So how do we facilitate a new way of political thinking? Diversify the conversation in the media, giving space to environmental crises other than climate change that are less likely to benefit from linear, technological solutions that fit within our current economic frameworks. Talking seriously about fringe solutions like intergenerational justice and degrowth is equally important. In our education system, we can shift the focus from "developing human capital" to "fostering imaginative potential." And we can fight for voting rights, perhaps even try to bring proportional representation into our politics, to allow pockets of imagination of alternative futures to enter the political mainstream.

About the Author

Peter Sutoris is an environmental anthropologist and lecturer (assistant professor) at the University of York. He's the author of Visions of Development *(Oxford University Press) and* Educating for the Anthropocene *(MIT Press). He tweets @Psutoris and his research can be found at www.petersutoris.com.*

These Alternative Economies Are Inspirations for a Sustainable World

By Ashish Kothari

No one in her village faced food shortages during the lockdowns, nor did they suffer from COVID-19, Moligeri Chandramma assured me through an interpreter this past March. A farmer in the drylands of southern India, she grows more than 40 species and varieties of crops—mostly native millets, rice, lentils and spices—on a bit more than a hectare of land. Chandramma is a member of the Deccan Development Society (DDS), a cooperative of nearly 5,000 Dalit (oppressed caste) and Adivasi (Indigenous) women whose remarkable integration of biodiversity conservation with agricultural livelihoods earned them the United Nations' prestigious Equator Award in 2019. Emerging from a situation of extreme malnutrition and social and gender discrimination in the 1980s, these farmers now enjoy food sovereignty and economic security. Not only are they weathering the pandemic, in 2020 each family in DDS contributed around 10 kilograms of food grains to the region's relief effort for those without land and livelihoods.

On the other side of the world, six Indigenous Quechua communities of the Peruvian Andes govern the Parque de la Papa (Potato Park) in Pisac, Cusco, a mountainous landscape that is one of the original homelands of the potato. They protect the region as a "biocultural heritage" territory, a trove of biological and cultural riches inherited from ancestors, and conserve more than 1,300 varieties of potato. When I visited in 2008 with other researchers and activists, I was stunned into silence by the diversity.

"This is the outcome of 20 years' consistent work in relocalizing our food system, from a time when we had become too dependent on outside agencies for our basic needs," farmer Mariano Sutta Apocusi told Local Futures, an organization dedicated to strengthening communities worldwide, in August 2020. "Focusing on the local has helped us improve access to and affordability of a great diversity of food products–especially native potatoes, quinoa, kiwicha, other Andean tubers and maize, which we cultivate using Indigenous agroecological methods." The communities instituted strong health and safety measures when the pandemic hit, even as they harvested a bumper crop and distributed more than a ton of potatoes to migrants, the elderly and a shelter for abused teenage mothers in Cusco town.

In Europe, many "solidarity economy" initiatives, which promote a culture of caring and sharing, swung into action when COVID-related lockdowns rendered massive numbers of people jobless. In Lisbon, Portugal, the social centers Disgraa and RDA69, which strive to re-create community life in an otherwise highly fragmented urban situation, reached out with free or cheap food to whoever needed it. They provided not only meals but also spaces where refugees, the homeless, unemployed young people and others who might otherwise have fallen through the cracks could interact with and develop relationships with better-off families, creating a social-security network of sorts. The organizers trusted those with adequate means to donate food or funds to the effort, strengthening the feeling of community in surrounding neighborhoods.

The pandemic has exposed the brittleness of a globalized economy that is advertised as benefiting everyone but in fact creates deep inequalities and insecurities. In India alone, 75 million people fell below the poverty line in 2020; globally, hundreds of millions who depend for their survival and livelihoods on the long-distance trade and exchange of goods and services were badly hit. Similar, albeit less extreme, dislocations also appeared during the 2008 financial crisis, when commodity speculation, along with the diversion of food grains to biofuel production, precipitated a steep rise in global grain prices, leading to hunger and food riots in many countries that depended on imported food. Threats to survival also emerge when war or other dislocations stop the movement of goods. In such crises, communities fare better if they have local markets and services and can provide their own food, energy and water while taking care of the less fortunate.

The value of these alternative ways of living goes far beyond their resilience during relatively short-term upheavals like the pandemic, however. As a researcher and environmental activist based in a "developing" country, I have long advocated that the worldviews of peoples who live close to nature be incorporated into global strategies for wildlife protection, such as at the International Union for Conservation of Nature and the United Nations' Convention on Biological Diversity. And in recent decades I have come to agree with critics of globalization such as social scientist and environmentalist Wolfgang Sachs that fending off calamities like biodiversity collapse will require not only environmental adaptations but also radical changes to the dominant economic, social and even political paradigms.

In 2014 a few of us in India initiated a process to explore pathways to a world in which people are at peace with one another and with nature. Five years later (and fortuitously, just before the pandemic hit), the endeavor grew into an international online network we called the Global Tapestry of Alternatives. These conversations and other research indicate that viable options, no matter where they are, tend to be based on self-reliance and solidarity.

Such values are at odds with globalization, which delivers to denizens of the Global North (the better off, no matter where we live) many things that we have come to regard as essential. In contrast to the promise of ever increasing material wealth that underpins our civilization, peoples who live near or beyond its margins have a multitude of visions for living well, each tailored to the specifics of their ecosystems and cultures. To walk away from the cliff edge of irreversible destabilization of the biosphere, I believe we must enable alternative structures, such as those of the Dalit farmers, the Quechua conservers and the Lisbon volunteers, to flourish and link up into a tapestry that ultimately covers the globe.

An Enlightening Journey

Growing up in India, where lifestyles that are intimately entwined with the natural environment survive in large pockets, unquestionably influenced my ideas of what constitutes true sustainability. In the 1970s, as a high school student who loved bird-watching in forests around Delhi, I joined classmates to demonstrate outside the Saudi Arabian embassy when some princes arrived in the country to hunt the (now critically endangered) Great Indian Bustard. Our protest, along with that of the Bishnoi community in Rajasthan, which traditionally protects these birds and other wildlife, embarrassed the Indian government into requesting that the hunters go home. Many of us went on to campaign for protection of the Delhi Ridge Forest, one of the world's biggest urban jungles. In 1979 we formed an environmental group to systematize our efforts. We called it Kalpavriksh, after a mythical tree that makes wishes come true; the name symbolized our growing awareness that nature gives us everything.

Our activism would teach us at least as much as we learned in school and college. While investigating the sources of Delhi's air pollution, for instance, we interviewed villagers who lived around a coal-fired power plant just outside the city. They turned out to be far worse affected by its dust and pollution than we city dwellers were–although they got none of its electricity. The benefits of the project flowed mainly to those who were already better off, whereas the disempowered experienced most of the harms.

In late 1980 we traveled to the western Himalayans to meet the protagonists of the iconic Chipko movement. Since 1973 village women had been protecting trees slated for logging by the forest department or by companies based in the Indian plains with their bodies. The deodars being felled, as well as the oaks, rhododendrons, and other species, were sacred, the women told us, as well as being essential for their survival. They provided cattle fodder, fertilizer and wild foods and sustained their water sources. Even as an urban student, I could see the central role that rural women played in protecting the environment–as well as the injustice of distant bureaucrats making decisions with little concern for how they impacted those on the ground.

Soon after, my friends and I learned that 30 major dams were to be constructed on the Narmada River basin in central India. Millions worshipped the Narmada as a tempestuous but bountiful goddess–so pristine that the Ganga is believed to visit her every year to wash away her sins. Trekking, boating and riding buses along its length of 1,300 kilometers, we were dazzled by waterfalls plunging into spectacular gorges, densely forested slopes teeming with wildlife, fields of diverse crops, thriving villages and ancient temples, all of which would be drowned. We began to question the concept of development itself. Surely the destruction would far outweigh any possible benefits? Almost four decades later our fears have proved tragically true. Hundreds of thousands of displaced people still await proper rehabilitation, and the river downstream of the dams has become a trickle–enabling seawater to reach 100 kilometers inland.

Over the years I came to understand how powerful economic forces reach around the globe to intimately link social injustice with ecological destruction. The era of colonization and slavery vastly expanded the economic and military reach of some nation-states and their allied corporations, enabling the worldwide extraction of natural resources and exploitation of labor to feed the emerging industrial revolution in Europe and North America. Economic historians, anthropologists and others have demonstrated how this painful history laid the foundation of today's global economy. Apart from driving irreversible ecological damage, this economic system robs many communities of access to the commons–to rivers, meadows and forests essential for their survival–while creating a dependence on external markets. The massive suffering during the pandemic has merely exposed these historical and contemporary fault lines.

During my wanderings over the decades and especially while researching a book with economist Aseem Shrivastava, I became aware of a far more hopeful trend. Across the country and indeed around the world, hundreds of social movements are empowering the marginalized to wrest back control over their lives and livelihoods. In 2014 Kalpavriksh initiated a series of gatherings called Vikalp Sangam, or Confluence of Alternatives, where the drivers of these spirited efforts could come together, share ideas and experiences, and collaborate, helping to build a critical mass for change.

These interactions and eclectic reading gave me insights into a vital question I was investigating: What are the essential characteristics of desirable and viable alternatives? Happily, I was far from alone in this quest. At a degrowth conference in Leipzig in 2014, I was excited to hear Alberto Acosta, an economist and former politician from Ecuador, speaking on *buen vivir,* an Indigenous worldview founded on living well with one another and with the rest of nature. Although Acosta spoke no English and I spoke no Spanish, we tried excitedly to converse; subsequently, degrowth expert Federico Demario joined us and helped to translate. We decided to work on a compilation of thriving alternatives from around the world–jotting down 20 possible ideas on the back of an envelope. Later we roped in development critic Arturo Escobar and ecofeminist Ariel Salleh as co-editors of a volume we called *Pluriverse*. The number of entries expanded to more than 100.

Commonalities

Though dazzlingly diverse, the alternatives emerging worldwide share certain core principles. The most important is sustaining or reviving community governance of the commons–of land, ecosystems, seeds, water and knowledge. In 12th-century England, powerful people began fencing off, or "enclosing," fields, meadows, forests and streams that had hitherto been used by all. Enclosures by landlords and industrialists expanded to Europe and accelerated with the industrial revolution, forcing tens of millions of dispossessed people to either become factory workers or emigrate to the New World, devastating native populations. Imperial nations seized large portions of continents and reconfigured the economies of the colonies, extracting raw materials for factories, capturing markets for exports of manufactured goods and obtaining foods such as wheat, sugar and tea for the newly created working class. In this way, colonizers and their allies established a system of perpetual economic domination that generated the Global North and the Global South (the world of the marginalized, no matter where they live).

The wave of anticolonial movements in the first few decades of the 20th century, many of them successful, sparked fears that supplies of raw materials for industries and markets for finished goods of higher value would dry up. President Harry S. Truman responded by launching a program for alleviating poverty in what he described as "underdeveloped areas" with their "primitive and stagnant" economies. As detailed by ecologist Debal Deb, newly formed financial institutions controlled by the rich countries helped the ex-colonies "develop" along the path blazed by the West, providing the materials and energy sources for and creating markets for cars, refrigerators and other consumer goods. An integral aspect of development, as thus conceived, propagated and usually enforced by stringent conditions attached to loans from the World Bank and the International Monetary Fund, has been privatization or state confiscation of the commons to extract metals, oil and water.

As Elinor Ostrom, winner of the 2009 Nobel Memorial Prize in Economic Sciences, demonstrated, however, the commons are far more sustainably governed by the communities from which they are wrested than by the governments or corporations that claim them. This awareness has given rise to innumerable grassroots efforts to protect the surviving commons and reestablish control over others. What constitutes the commons has also expanded to include "physical and knowledge resources that we all share for everyone's benefit," explains sociologist Ana Margarida Esteves, who helps with the European Commons Assembly, an umbrella organization for hundreds of such endeavors.

Many of the efforts resemble the DDS and the Parque de la Papa in using community governance of commonly held resources to enhance agroecology (smallholder farming that sustains soil, water and biodiversity) and food sovereignty (control over all means of food production, including land, soil, seeds and the knowledge of how to use them). The food-sovereignty movement La Via Campesina, which originated in Brazil in 1993, now includes about 200 million farmers in 81 countries. Such attempts at self-reliance and community governance extend also to other basic needs, such as for energy and water. In Costa Rica, Spain and Italy, rural cooperatives have been generating electricity locally and controlling its distribution since the 1990s. And hundreds of villages in western India have moved toward "water democracy," based on decentralized harvesting of water and community management of wetlands and groundwater. Mobilizing people to sustain, build or rebuild local systems of knowledge is essential to such ventures.

Secure rights to govern the commons are also important. In the Ecuadorian Amazon, the Sapara Indigenous people fought hard to gain collective rights over their rain-forest home. They are now defending it against oil and mining interests while developing a model of economic well-being that blends their traditional cosmovisions–ways of knowing, being and doing that are physically and spiritually linked to their environs–with new activities such as community-led ecotourism. Their income from tourism has dropped during the pandemic, but their forests and community ethic give them almost all the food, water, energy, housing, medicines, enjoyment, health and learning that they need. They are now offering online sessions on their cosmovisions, dream analysis and healing. I participated in such sessions in person in their Naku ecotourism camp in 2019. The virtual version is not as immersive but nonetheless represents an innovative adaptation to the circumstances.

Greening cities or making them more welcoming, as the Lisbon social centers do, also requires community-based governance and economies of caring and sharing. Across the Global South, development projects have driven hundreds of millions of people to cities, where they live in slums and work in hazardous conditions. Wealthy city dwellers could do their part by consuming less, which would reduce the extraction and waste dumping that displace people in faraway places. A spectrum of avenues toward more equitable and sustainable cities has emerged. These include, for example, the Transition Movement, which is attempting to regenerate the commons and make European cities carbon-neutral, and the municipalism movement, which is creating a network of Fearless Cities, among them Barcelona, Valparaiso, Madrid and Athens, to provide secure environments for refugees and migrants. Urban agriculture in Havana supplies more than half of its fresh food requirements and has inspired many other city farming initiatives around the world.

Five Petals

These initiatives point to the need for fundamental transformations in five interconnected realms. In the *economic sphere*, we need to get away from the development paradigm–including the notion that economic growth, as measured by gross domestic product (GDP), is the best means of achieving human goals. In its place, we need systems for respecting ecological limits, emphasizing well-being in all its dimensions and localizing exchanges to enable self-reliance–as well as good measures of these indicators. Bhutan has long experimented with gross national happiness as an index; the idea has spawned variants, such as New Zealand's recent focus on mental health and other such measures of progress.

We also need freedom from centralized monetary and financial control. Many experiments in alternative currencies and economies based on trust and local exchanges are underway. Perhaps the most innovative of these is "time banking," a system for swapping services founded on the principle that all skills or occupations merit equal respect. One can, for example, give a one-hour-long yoga lesson for credit that can be redeemed for an hour's work on bicycle repair.

In many parts of the world, workers are seeking to control the means of production: land, nature, knowledge and tools. A few years back I visited Vio.Me, a detergent factory in Thessaloniki, Greece, which workers had taken over and converted from chemical to olive-oil-based and eco-friendly production, and where they had established complete parity in pay, regardless of what job the worker was doing. The slogan on their wall proclaimed: "We have no boss!"

In fact, work itself is being redefined. Globalized modernity has created a chasm between work and leisure—which is why we wait desperately for the weekend! Many movements seek to bridge this gap, enabling greater enjoyment, creativity and satisfaction. In industrial countries, people are bringing back manual ways of making clothes, footwear or processed foods under banners such as "The future is handmade!" In western India, many young people are leaving soul-killing routines in factories to return to handloom weaving, which allows them to control their schedules while providing a creative outlet.

In the *political sphere*, the centralization of power inherent in the nation-state, whether democratic or authoritarian, disempowers many peoples. The Sapara nation in Ecuador and the Adivasis of central India argue for a more direct democracy, where power resides primarily with the community. The state—insofar as it continues to exist—would then mainly help with larger-scale coordination while being strictly accountable to decision-making units on the ground. The ancient Indian notion of *swaraj*, literally translated as "self-rule," is particularly relevant here. It emphasizes individual and collective autonomy and freedom that are linked to responsibility for others' autonomy and freedom. A community that practices *swaraj* may not dam a stream, for example, if that threatens the water supply of downstream villages; its well-being cannot compromise that of others.

Such a notion of democracy also challenges the boundaries of nation-states, many of which are products of colonial history and have ruptured ecologically and culturally contiguous areas. The Kurdish people, for instance, are split among Turkey, Iran, Iraq and Syria. For three decades they have struggled to achieve autonomy and direct democracy based on principles of ecological sustainability and women's liberation—and without borders dividing them. And Indigenous groups in Mexico collectively identifying as

Zapatistas have for more than three decades asserted and sustained an autonomous region based on similar principles.

Moving toward such radical democracy would suggest a world with far fewer borders, weaving tens of thousands of relatively autonomous and self-reliant communities into a tapestry of alternatives. These societies would connect with one another through "horizontal" networks of equitable and respectful exchange, as well as through "vertical" but downwardly accountable institutions that manage processes and activities across the landscape.

Several experiments in bioregionalism at large scales are underway, although most remain somewhat top-down in their governance. In Australia, the Great Eastern Ranges Initiative seeks to coordinate the conservation of ecosystems across 3,600 kilometers while sustaining livelihoods and community health. And a project spanning six countries in the Andes aims to conserve as a World Heritage Site the Qhapaq an, a 30,000-kilometer network of roads built by the Inca Empire, along with its related cultural, historical and environmental heritage.

Local self-governance may, of course, be oppressive or exclusionary. The intensely patriarchal and casteist traditional village councils in many parts of India and the xenophobic antirefugee approaches of the right wing in Europe illustrate this drawback. A third crucial sphere of transformation is therefore *social justice,* encompassing struggles against racism, casteism, patriarchy, and other traditional or modern forms of discrimination and exploitation. Fortunately, success in defying the dominant economic system often goes hand in hand with victories against discrimination, such as Dalit women farmers' shaking off centuries of caste and patriarchal oppression to achieve food sovereignty.

Political autonomy and economic self-reliance need not mean isolationism and xenophobia. Rather cultural and material exchanges that maintain local self-reliance and respect ecological sustainability would replace present-day globalization—which perversely allows goods and finances to flow freely but stops desperate humans at borders. This kind of localization would be open to people in need;

refugees from climate change or war would be welcomed, as in the network of Fearless Cities in Europe. Both grounded practice and shifts in policy could help transit toward such a system. Necessary, of course, are attempts to rebuild societies in regions of strife so that people do not have to flee from them.

Radical change also necessitates transformations in a fourth sphere: that of *culture and knowledge*. Globalization devalues languages, cultures and knowledge systems that do not adapt to development. Several movements are confronting this homogenizing tendency. The Sapara nation is trying to resuscitate its almost extinct language and preserve its knowledge of the forest by bringing these into the curriculum of the local school, for instance. Many communities are "decolonizing" maps, putting back their own place names and defying political borders. Even the colonial-era Mercator projection used to generate the familiar world map is being upended. (Only recently did I realize that Africa is large enough to contain Europe, China, the U.S. and India put together.) Increasingly, traditional and modern sciences are collaborating to help solve humankind's most vexing problems. The Arctic Biodiversity Assessment, for example, involves cooperation among Indigenous peoples and university scientists to tackle climate change.

One problem is that present-day educational institutions train graduates who are equipped to serve and perpetuate the dominant economic system. People are bringing community and nature back into spaces of learning, however. These efforts include Forest Schools in many parts of Europe that provide children with hands-on learning in the midst of nature, the Zapatista autonomous schools that teach about diverse cultures and struggles, and the Ecoversities Alliance of centers of higher learning around the world that enable scholars to seek knowledge across the boundaries that typically separate academic disciplines.

The most important sphere of transformation, however, is the ecological–recognizing that we are part of nature and that other species are worthy of respect in their own right. Across the Global South, communities are leading efforts to regenerate degraded ecosystems and wildlife populations and conserve biodiversity. Tens of thousands of "territories of life" are being governed by Indigenous or other local communities, for example. These include locally managed marine areas in the South Pacific, Indigenous territories in Latin America and Australia, community forests in South Asia, and the Ancestral Domain territories in the Philippines. Also noteworthy is recent legislation or court judgments in several countries asserting that rivers, for example, enjoy the same protections as people. The United Nations' 2009 Declaration on Harmony with Nature is an important milestone toward such a goal.

Values

I am often asked how one scales up successful alternatives. It would be self-defeating, however, to try to either scale up or replicate a DDS or a Parque de la Papa. The essence of this approach is diversity: the recognition that every situation is different. What people can do–and this, indeed, is how successful initiatives spread–is understand the underlying values and apply these in their own communities while networking with like ventures to spread the impact.

The Vikalp Sangam process has identified the following values as crucial: solidarity, dignity, interconnectedness, rights and responsibilities, diversity, autonomy and freedom, self-reliance and self-determination, simplicity, nonviolence and respect for all life. Around the world both ancient and modern worldviews that are focused on life articulate similar principles. Indigenous peoples and other local communities have lived by worldviews such as *buen vivir*, *swaraj*, *ubuntu* (an African philosophy that sees the well-being of all living things as interconnected) and many other such ethical systems for centuries and are reasserting them. Simultaneously, approaches such as degrowth and ecofeminism have emerged from within industrial societies, seeding powerful countercultures.

At the heart of these worldviews lies a simple principle: that we are all holders of power. That in the exercise of this power, we not only assert our own autonomy and freedom but also are responsible for ensuring the autonomy of others. Such a *swaraj* merges with ecological sustainability to create an eco-*swaraj*, encompassing respect for all life.

Clearly, such fundamental transformations face a deeply entrenched status quo that retaliates violently wherever it perceives a threat. Hundreds of environmental defenders are murdered every year. Another serious challenge is the unfamiliarity many people in the Global North have with ideals of a good life beyond the American dream. Even so, the fact that many progressive initiatives are thriving and new ones are sprouting suggests that a combination of resistance and constructive alternatives does stand a chance.

The COVID pandemic is a catastrophe that presents humankind with a choice. Will we head right back toward some semblance of the old normal, or will we adopt new pathways out of global ecological and social crises? To maximize the likelihood of the latter, we need to go well beyond the Green New Deal approaches in the U.S., Europe, and elsewhere. Their intense focus on the climate crisis and worker rights is valuable, but we also need to challenge unsustainable consumption patterns, glaring inequalities and the need for centralized nation-states.

Truly life-sustaining recoveries would emphasize all the spheres of eco-*swaraj*, arrived at via four pathways. One is the creation or revival of dignified, secure and self-reliant livelihoods for two billion people based on collective governance of natural resources and small-scale production processes such as farming, fisheries, crafts, manufacturing and services. Another is a program for regeneration and conservation of ecosystems, led by Indigenous peoples and local communities. A third is immediate public investments in health, education, transportation, housing, energy and other basic needs, planned and delivered by local democratic governance. Finally, incentives and disincentives to make production and consumption patterns sustainable are crucial. These approaches would integrate sustainability, equality and diversity, giving everyone, especially the most marginalized, a voice. A proposal for a million climate jobs in South Africa is of this nature, as is a feminist recovery plan for Hawaii and several other proposals for social justice in other countries.

None of this will be easy, but I believe it is essential if we are to make peace with Earth and among ourselves.

About the Author

Ashish Kothari is a founding member of Kalpavriksh, an environmental organization in India. He helps coordinate the Global Tapestry of Alternatives and has co-authored or co-edited several books, including Churning the Earth *(2012) and* Pluriverse *(2019).*

Fossil-Fuel Subsidies Must End

By Geoffrey Supran, Peter Erickson, Doug Koplow, Michael Lazarus, Peter Newell, Naomi Oreskes, Harro van Asselt

When it comes to tackling the climate crisis, ending $400 billion in annual subsidies to the fossil-fuel industry worldwide seems like a no-brainer. For the past decade world leaders have been resolving and reaffirming the need to phase them out. All the 2020 Democratic presidential candidates committed to eliminating fossil-fuel subsidies, and the vast majority of the American public supports doing so. International financial institutions such as the World Bank and International Monetary Fund have joined the chorus, pointing to the benefits of reform.

In 2018, however, a group of researchers questioned the magnitude of the climate benefits of subsidy reform, reporting that their simulations showed its effect would be "limited" and "small." Stories in the press began asking whether such subsidies are such a big deal after all.

We think this is wrong. In a paper in February in the journal *Nature*, we make the case that they do matter–a lot. In the 2018 study, emissions reductions from subsidy removal were calculated by the researchers to be 500 million to two billion metric tons of carbon dioxide a year by 2030. This figure is by no means "small." It amounts to roughly one quarter of the energy-related emissions reductions pledged by all the countries participating in the Paris Agreement (four billion to eight billion metric tons). Hundreds of millions of metric tons of CO2 reductions is nothing to sneeze at, particularly when it can be achieved by a single policy approach that also brings strong fiscal, environmental and health benefits.

Moreover, previous work has more than likely underestimated the emissions reductions that would occur because commonly used techniques do not accurately capture the investment dynamics of fossil fuels. But these dynamics can greatly affect what oil and gas companies do.

In our analysis of the issue, we take the example of one specific subsidy: a federal tax break that allows U.S. oil producers to immediately deduct from their taxes most of the costs of constructing and drilling new wells. Conventional models assume that such subsidies are uniformly distributed across all oil fields, whereas in reality, governments often preferentially target new—rather than existing—capital investments. The result is a lowering of producers' up-front cash-flow requirements, leading them to drill more new wells than they otherwise would. This process locks in and accelerates fossil-fuel production and, in turn, greenhouse gas emissions. We estimate that true emissions reductions from eliminating this tax-break subsidy could be more than an order of magnitude greater than was predicted using the conventional modeling approach.

And this tax break is just one subsidy. A separate, peer-reviewed analysis by some of us in 2017 demonstrated that without a dozen key subsidies, nearly half of U.S. future oil production could be unprofitable at $50-per-barrel oil prices—the level at which prices may hover in a low-carbon future.

In other countries, the forms of subsidies can, of course, vary. But around the world, fossil-fuel production and consumption are supported in hundreds of ways. Indeed, the most troubling impact and legacy of fossil-fuel subsidies may be the political barriers—rather than financial ones—that fossil-fuel producers have erected against decarbonization efforts over a period of decades. Revenue boosts from subsidies can support not only more drilling but also product promotion, political activities and other efforts that reinforce the industry's incumbent status. Subsidies also have a symbolic effect, signaling that this industry and its activities are beneficial for society as a whole and that they therefore should be encouraged.

In another paper, published in a February issue of the *Proceedings of the National Academy of Sciences USA*, experts studying the social tipping points for climate stabilization concluded that "redirecting national subsidy programs to renewables ... or removing the subsidies for fossil-fuel technologies are the tipping interventions that are needed for the takeoff and diffusion of fossil-fuel-free energy systems."

Economic models provide useful guidance to policy makers. But as we show in our article, most have a blind spot, failing to capture key ways in which subsidies send signals to markets and people. Overreliance on these models can create a false sense of certainty that misses the big picture: of course, subsidies matter to the fossil-fuel industry and help to prop it up. That is why they were introduced in the first place and why the industry and its allies continue to defend them. As the Department of Energy itself concluded 40 years ago, federal subsidies have had a "large effect" on capital formation and oil production in the U.S. And more oil infrastructure and more production mean more greenhouse gas emissions.

The public and policy makers should be under no illusions about the basic realities at stake: Holding back catastrophic global warming requires dramatically reducing fossil-fuel production. And subsidies to fossil-fuel companies undermine that goal. Once upon a time, it made sense for countries to support their fossil-fuel industries. But that time is over.

This was originally published as an opinion piece. The views expressed are those of the author(s) and are not necessarily those of Scientific American.

About the Authors

Geoffrey Supran is a research associate in the Department of the History of Science at Harvard University.

Peter Erickson is a senior scientist at the Stockholm Environment Institute.

Doug Koplow is founder of Earth Track in Cambridge, Mass.

Michael Lazarus is a senior scientist at the Stockholm Environment Institute.

Peter Newell is a professor of international relations at the University of Sussex in England.

Naomi Oreskes is a professor of the history of science at Harvard University. She is author of Why Trust Science? *(Princeton University Press, 2019) and co-author of* Discerning Experts *(University of Chicago, 2019).*

Section 5: Can Technology Halt Climate Change?

The Economist Takes a Strange Turn on Science

By Tali Trigg

In recent issues of *The Economist*, a strange habit has popped up: a reliance on a controversial climate skeptic for scientific climate consensus. Said scientist, Bjorn Lomborgh, known to many for pushing climate skepticism and presenting climate change mitigation and the fight against HIV/Aids as an "either-or scenario," has somehow become the go-to source for climate change analysis in *The Economist*, an otherwise reasonable magazine.

In a recent climate special – coming on the heels of the successful climate conference held in Paris this past December – *The Economist* took a closer look at geoengineering as a potential option for avoiding climate catastrophe; the basic idea being that instead of preventing global greenhouse gases, could we instead reverse the effects?

While there are many open questions about this approach, including from an ethical point-of-view, the biggest problem with geoengineering is that it assumes we can foresee or accurately model the consequences of any global intervention; something we are really not good at doing.

None of this comes across when reading *The Economist*'s take on it, as one is instead told that, *"...[a] report published in 2012 for the Copenhagen Consensus Centre estimated that marine-cloud brightening would prevent global warming even more effectively than a carbon tax."*

From this questionable finding you might infer that the Copenhagen Consensus Centre is a go-to source for reliable scientific research, yet it was shut down back in 2012 mired in controversy, and remains mired in said controversies as it tries to open an office in Australia.

The mischievously named Copenhagen Consensus Centre does not represent a consensus as much as an outlier of climate skepticism. Lomborgh states, *"A lot of poor countries are going to get a lot richer by burning fossil fuels,"* a long-held belief of climate skeptics, namely that taking action on climate change is equal to forcing developing nations to stay developing.

Instead, fighting climate change might actually help combat e.g. malaria, but dismissing climate change mitigation until malaria and other major issues are taken care of first is disingenuous. Further, it is a false premise at best, and a dangerous ignorance of systems effects at its worst.

Which brings us back to geoengineering. While it is too soon to dismiss geoengineering outright (and not because it is politically incorrect as Lomborgh and others might have you believe), its risks and uncertain rewards need to be weighed against existing solutions to solving climate change e.g. solar power and its plummeting costs.

For a levelheaded and peer-reviewed take on the complexities and lack of answers relating to geoengineering, *The Economist* may instead want to drop Lomborgh and his "*Consensus*" for others e.g. Bellamy et al 2012, Caldeira et al 2013 or Pacific Northwest National Laboratory.

This was originally published as an opinion piece. The views expressed are those of the author(s) and are not necessarily those of Scientific American.

About the Author

Tali Trigg is an energy analyst, technology policy advisor and writer. His work includes research and analysis on energy and transportation, with an emphasis on the role of cities in shaping transport energy demand and mobility solutions. His blog covers the wide range of mobility and energy, with deep-dives into numbers and maps, but is keen to cover anything transport-related and under-reported. Opinions are his own.

The Best Technology for Fighting Climate Change Isn't a Technology

By Han de Groot

The latest IPCC report does not mince words about the state of our planet: we must act now to achieve global change at a scale that has "no documented historical precedent" in order to avoid the climate catastrophe that would result from a 2 degree C rise in average global temperature. Climate change already disproportionately affects the world's most vulnerable people including poor rural communities that depend on the land for their livelihoods and coastal communities throughout the tropics. Indeed, we have already seen the stark asymmetry of suffering resulting from extreme weather events, such as hurricanes, floods, droughts, wildfires and more.

So far, advocates and politicians have tended to focus on reducing fossil fuel consumption through technology and/or policy, such as a steep carbon tax, as climate solutions. These proposals are, of course, essential to reducing manmade carbon emissions–71 percent of which are generated by just 100 fossil fuel companies. For this reason, fossil-fuel–related emissions reductions rightly figure heavily in the national climate commitments of the 181 nations that signed the global Paris Agreement.

Yet the international focus on fossil fuels has overshadowed the most powerful and cost-efficient carbon-capture technology the world has yet seen: forests. Recent scientific research confirms that forests and other "natural climate solutions" are absolutely essential in mitigating climate change, thanks to their carbon sequestering and storage capabilities. In fact, natural climate solutions can help us achieve 37 percent of our climate target, even though they currently receive only 2.5 percent of public climate financing.

Forests' power to store carbon dioxide through the simple process of tree growth is staggering: one tree can store an average of about 48 pounds of carbon dioxide in one year. Recent research shows intact forests are capable of storing the equivalent of the carbon dioxide emissions of entire countries such as Peru and Colombia.

For this reason, policy makers and business leaders must create and enforce ambitious policies and incentives to prevent deforestation, foster reforestation of degraded land, and support the sustainable management of standing forests in the fight against climate change. Protecting the world's forests ensures they can continue to provide essential functions aside from climate stability, including producing oxygen, filtering water and supporting biodiversity. Not only do all the world's people depend on forests to provide clean air, clean water, oxygen, and medicines, but 1.6 billion people rely on them directly for their livelihoods.

Unfortunately, we are fighting a crisis of deforestation, much of it driven by conversion to agricultural lands to produce a handful of resource-intensive commodities, despite zero-deforestation commitments from companies and governments. With increasing atmospheric carbon dioxide, insufficient emissions reductions and continued high rates of deforestation, urgent action is needed to avoid the worst effects of climate change.

Now is the time to increase investment in and attention to forest protection and restoration. In doing so, we will also address a number of other pressing global issues. For example, increasing tree cover can help address the problem of food security in many areas. Trees can enhance farm productivity and provide farmers with another source of revenue through the sale of fruits, nuts or timber—all while storing carbon dioxide. It is estimated that increased investment in the multi-strata agroforestry area could help sequester up to 9.28 gigatons of carbon dioxide, while saving a net $709.8 billion by 2050. In production landscapes where large-scale tree cover increases are difficult, agroforestry serves as an attractive compromise.

And in less-developed, rural areas—especially in the tropics—community-based sustainable forest management programs can provide pathways out of poverty. In the Petén region of Guatemala, for instance, community-managed forests have boasted a near-zero deforestation rate over the past 14 years, as compared to 12 percent in nearby protected areas and buffer zones. These communities have built low-impact, sustainable forest-based businesses that have bolstered the economy of the region enough to fund the creation of local schools and health services. Their success is especially poignant in a region otherwise besieged by deforestation; outside the community-managed zones, deforestation rates increase by 20x.

Finally, landscape restoration promises an unparalleled return on investment, in terms of ecosystem services and carbon sequestered and stored. Landscape restoration could potentially sequester up to 1.7 gigatons of carbon dioxide every year, according to the International Union for Conservation of Nature. Reforestation projects can also intersect neatly and positively with human systems—restored forests provide a renewed resource base and new economic opportunities for communities.

There is good work being done on this front already. The Bonn Challenge, issued by world leaders with the goal of reforestation and restoration of 150 million hectares of degraded landscapes by 2020, has been adopted by 56 countries. Many governments and groups pledged to halve global deforestation by 2020 through the New York Declaration on Forests. And in an exemplary display of public-private sector cooperation, the Cocoa and Forests Initiative in Cote d'Ivoire and Ghana aims to end deforestation from cocoa cultivation.

With world leaders gathering in December for their yearly U.N. climate talks, the time is ripe for concrete action on forests and natural climate solutions. World leaders now have the opportunity to make big gains on climate by dramatically ramping up their investment in proven, natural solutions. More trees in the ground. More reforestation projects. More sustainable forestry. More avoided deforestation through sustainable agriculture and certified crops.

We can't afford to wait.

This was originally published as an opinion piece. The views expressed are those of the author(s) and are not necessarily those of Scientific American.

Can Natural Gas Be Part of a Low-Carbon Future?

By Michael E. Webber

In the mid-2010s it became common to say that natural gas would be a bridge fuel to a zero-carbon future, in which solar, wind and other renewable technologies provide all of our energy without any carbon dioxide emissions to worsen climate change. But if natural gas is really a bridge, then it's not part of the long-term plan. And if we actually build the bridge, we're likely to stay on it.

Natural gas consumption in the U.S. has risen by a third in the past 15 years. Gas accounts for 32 percent of total energy consumption and is now the biggest source of electricity nationwide, largely displacing coal-fired power plants. Natural gas—primarily methane—burns much cleaner than coal does, and it provides ready backup to variable wind and solar farms. That sounds promising, except burning natural gas still creates CO2. Methane in wells and pipelines can leak into the atmosphere, amplifying global warming. And once the last coal plant closes, natural gas plants become the dirtiest electricity sources.

To reduce CO2 emissions, society has to decarbonize its energy systems as quickly as possible. Building more wind and solar farms is relatively inexpensive and fast, and it accelerates the shutdown of coal plants. But exploiting the best locations—the windswept plains and sunbaked deserts—requires a greatly expanded transmission grid to bring the electrons to major cities and manufacturing complexes. Those wires and poles introduce risks from windstorms, floods and fires—all rising because of climate change—and township after township routinely fights expansion plans: "Not in my backyard."

The natural gas infrastructure, almost all belowground, is far less prone to interruption. The U.S. has about three million miles of natural gas pipelines running underneath nearly every major city in the contiguous 48 states. After adding all the compressors, tanks and storage caverns, the infrastructure is worth several trillion dollars. The power plants themselves add hundreds of billions of dollars more. The nearly 70 million households served by natural gas have furnaces, water heaters and cooktops worth at least another $100 billion. Multiply all that sunk investment by about five for the entire world. Gas is also more intertwined than any other energy source with other sectors of society–transportation, buildings (for heating and cooking) and industry (for heat and as a feedstock for chemicals)–making it harder to replace.

Swapping out that infrastructure before its natural lifetime ends would also entail financial losses for the current owners, who will push back. The replacement technology could cost taxpayers, ratepayers and homeowners, who will push back, too. And more electricity does not readily solve the need for liquid fuels burned in trucks, ships and planes or for intense heat in industrial foundries, distilleries and refineries that make volumes of metals, cement, glass, jet fuel and chemicals. The energy density of liquid fuels is difficult to match.

If we can clean emissions out of the natural gas system, it could be part of a carbon-neutral future instead of a bridge. The technology exists to extract the carbon or to transform the gas so that carbon coming out and carbon going in balance to zero or near zero.

The first step in a comprehensive plan for decarbonizing the nation's energy infrastructure would be improving energy efficiency and conservation to reduce consumption. The second would be to electrify as many cars, space heaters, water heaters and cooktops as is practical, using renewable sources. At the same time, tighten up the leaky gas infrastructure. And replace as much natural gas as possible with low-carbon alternatives such as biogas, hydrogen and synthesized methane or use a process called pyrolysis at the end of the natural gas pipes to get the carbon out.

Clean energy supporters rightly worry that any investment in gas infrastructure creates a lock-in effect. Each new power plant, pipeline or gas storage unit has an expected lifetime of 25 to 80 years, so each element could either become a trap for more emissions or a stranded asset. But we can solve the lock-in problem with drop-in alternatives to natural gas: low-carbon gases that can flow through existing pipes, tanks and power plants, taking advantage of those trillions of dollars of assets.

Zero-Carbon Gas

The drop-in substitute most ready for natural gas is biomethane—methane gas produced from biological sources. Microbes inside large drums called anaerobic digesters chew up organic matter such as crop waste, manure, sewage, and food waste and other garbage in landfills, producing methane. Biodigesters, already a mature technology, transform waste streams at landfills and the waste lagoons adjacent to concentrated animal feeding operations from environmental liabilities into valuable commodities, generating revenues for municipalities and farmers.

Biomethane is working in Austin, Tex. Waste Management, which operates one of the city's landfills, collects biomethane from 128 wells on its site and burns it to generate enough electricity for 4,000 to 6,000 homes. And one of the city's wastewater-treatment plants has eight biodigesters, each with two million gallons of capacity; microbes convert sewage into biogas that fuels on-site electricity generators. The process creates a solid by-product called Dillo Dirt, which feels and smells like a clumpy compost. A city contractor sells it by the bag in area stores to enrich soil.

About a quarter of the more than 2,000 U.S. landfills now harvest their gas or process their waste into biogas using biodigesters. That only offsets less than 1 percent of the country's total natural gas use, however. Biogas can serve as a direct substitute for natural gas, but the relative volume, globally, is low. If a farm, landfill or sewage plant cannot readily use the gas to make electricity or is not next to a gas grid, the biomethane might need to be liquefied and trucked to another location, reducing the carbon payoff. Still, biomethane is a commercially ready technology that can begin to decarbonize part of the gas system.

Hydrogen Instead of Methane

Natural gas can be replaced altogether, with hydrogen. Turbines can burn hydrogen to generate electricity for the grid, and internal-combustion engines can burn it in heavy-duty vehicles. Hydrogen in fuel cells can produce electricity for cars, homes or offices. And hydrogen is a ready building block for many basic chemicals. Burning it, or reacting it in fuel cells, does not produce CO2. Leaked hydrogen has a warming effect that is just a fraction of that of methane.

Natural hydrogen seeps out of the ground from basins in many cratons in the earth–large blocks of ancient rock that form the central parts of continents. Scientists have stumbled across these seeps for more than a century. Oil and gas companies, however, have considered hydrogen a nuisance when they find it alongside underground reservoirs because it can catch fire and can degrade metal piping. But today corporate and university researchers are drilling hydrogen test wells and launching multiyear programs to search for hydrogen underground. Anticipation feels similar to what arose during the very early days of fracking shale: a huge resource is out there, if engineers can figure out how to harness it cheaply and safely.

We can also manufacture hydrogen. Right now most hydrogen for industry is produced from steam re-forming of methane–adding heat and hot water to methane to create hydrogen and CO2. Electrolysis–using electricity to split water into hydrogen and oxygen–can also create hydrogen gas. Both processes require significant amounts of energy, however.

Moving and storing gaseous hydrogen is also a challenge. Because of hydrogen's low density, it takes a lot of energy to move it through a pipe compared with denser gases such as methane or liquids such as petroleum. After several hundred kilometers the inefficiency makes moving hydrogen more expensive than the value of the energy it carries. And hydrogen can embrittle steel pipelines unless that is mitigated by altering operating conditions or incorporating expensive alloys.

One way to integrate hydrogen is to mix it with methane in an existing natural gas pipeline. This blending decarbonizes some of the system by displacing a portion of the natural gas with hydrogen. Experiments in the U.K. and France show that a mixture of 80 percent methane and 20 percent hydrogen can be efficiently moved in a natural gas pipeline. As part of a study from mid-2018 to March 2020, Dunkirk, France, used an 80–20 blend to fuel 100 homes and a hospital boiler without any new equipment along the pipeline or in the buildings.

Fittings inside furnaces and stoves, such as burner tips, might need to be altered or replaced for blends with more than 20 percent hydrogen because, like pure hydrogen, blended gas burns at different temperatures and rates. Another consideration is that because of hydrogen's low energy density, a 20 percent blend by volume provides 14 percent less energy per cubic foot than natural gas.

One way around certain cost and safety challenges is to pipe hydrogen as part of another chemical form we know how to handle, such as ammonia, which has one nitrogen atom and three hydrogen atoms. Molecules that include hydrogen atoms are known as hydrogen carriers. Hydrogen is converted, where it is found or produced, into the carrier, which is dropped into existing pipelines, and is either used in that form or converted again into hydrogen at the destination.

Common carriers such as ammonia, formic acid and methanol are liquid at near-ambient conditions, making them easier to transport than gaseous hydrogen. Although ammonia is caustic, it is already moved worldwide as a fertilizer ingredient, and it can be burned without producing any CO2. Methane could be the most efficient option because it carries four hydrogen atoms for every carbon atom and is already compatible with existing pipes, compressors, tanks, turbines and appliances.

Demonstration projects are growing quickly in number. Finnish industrial builder Wärtsilä is constructing a new ship for 2023 named Viking Energy that will run on ammonia with fuel cells, avoiding greenhouse gas emissions and other pollutants that plague the maritime sector. Air France and the Charles De Gaulle airport in Paris are very interested in hydrogen as a way to decarbonize aviation. Hydrogen carriers are still in the early stages of research, however, so it is difficult to say how successful they could be.

Power plants that burn hydrogen are on drawing boards, too. In Delta, Utah, the Intermountain Power Plant–one of the largest U.S. coal-fired plants–sends electricity hundreds of miles to Los Angeles. To meet the city's long-term requirement for renewable and low-carbon energy, in 2025 plant owners will replace the coal boilers with turbines that can burn hydrogen. They will start with a blend of 30 percent hydrogen in natural gas and will shift to 100 percent hydrogen later. The hydrogen will be generated right there using electrolysis powered by wind and solar and will be stored in more than 100 existing, underground salt caverns, each about the size of the Empire State Building.

End of the Pipe

Instead of decarbonizing natural gas before it goes into the pipeline, we could remove the carbon at the end of the pipe, where customers consume the gas. Methane, for example, can be split at the user's location into hydrogen and solid carbon, which looks like a fine, black dust. The process, called methane pyrolysis, is efficient and eliminates CO2 emissions. Every kilogram of hydrogen produced from pyrolyzed methane generates three kilograms of solid carbon instead of nine kilograms of CO2 gas that would be emitted if the methane was burned.

The pile of carbon dust that accumulates inside a collector in a furnace or stove would be carted away each month or so. We already pay garbage haulers and municipal wastewater-processing plants to clean up our solid and liquid wastes; we should pay to clean up the waste from our gas use, too. The carbon piles actually have value, though, because they can be sold as a basic ingredient for making graphite, rubber, coatings, batteries and chemicals, as well as a soil amendment for agriculture.

Although engineers have studied methane pyrolysis for decades, they have deployed it only in small demonstration projects. Some equipment at the end of the pipe has to be changed to separate the carbon, but no expensive hydrogen pipelines would have to be built, simplifying matters greatly. Pyrolysis of conventional natural gas can bring the entire system to nearly zero carbon. Adding methane from biodigesters or made from CO2 in the atmosphere using renewable electricity could make the system carbon-negative.

Imagining any of these decarbonized futures might conjure up visions of large new industrial complexes or millions of small equipment changes for consumers. But so do other proposals to curb emissions. Electrifying every heater, stove and vehicle would require widespread technology replacement. Plans to directly pull CO2 from the air would require millions of big machines to capture the gas and sequester it–sprawling enterprises that would also demand lots of new land and new electricity.

Decarbonized gas would let us take advantage of trillions of dollars of existing pipelines, equipment and appliances, saving huge sums of money and years of time in creating a zero-carbon energy system. We would, of course, have to fix the leaky infrastructure. Leaks can be minimized by replacing pneumatic equipment with electric devices at well sites, improving the automation of pipe and tank inspections with sensors on drones and robots, and writing regulations that no longer turn a blind eye to leaking, as well as deliberately venting or burning unwanted gas. This work would create jobs for workers in the oil and gas industries and would clean up the energy infrastructure, which in turn could lessen pollution in communities near energy facilities.

Reining in climate change requires many solutions. Declaring who cannot be part of those, such as natural gas companies, only raises resistance to progress. Because decarbonized gas can complement renewable electricity and because it might be a faster, cheaper and more effective path for parts of society that are difficult to electrify, we should not discard gas as an option. We have a massive gas infrastructure, and we have to figure out what to do with it.

Scrapping it would be slow, expensive and incredibly difficult, but we could instead put it to work to help create a low-carbon future.

About the Author

Michael E. Webber is a professor of energy resources at the University of Texas at Austin and head of the Webber Energy Group there. He is also chief science and technology officer at ENGIE, a global energy and infrastructure firm in Paris that operates the world's largest independent electricity company as well as large natural gas networks.

New Nuclear Power Plants Are Unlikely to Stop the Climate Crisis

By Naomi Oreskes

Last fall my Harvard University class and I went through an exercise to help the students understand how the world might address the climate crisis and keep the average global temperature increase below two degrees Celsius. Guided by John Sterman, a management professor at the Massachusetts Institute of Technology, the students pretended to be climate negotiators, offering or blocking climate policies. Then, using En-ROADS, a computer simulation of the effects of climate policies that Sterman co-developed, they were able to see the consequences of their proposals on the 2100 average global temperature.

The exercise offered both bad news and good. The bad news is that keeping the rise in temperature below 2° C is going to be very hard and holding it under 1.5° probably impossible. The good news is that the challenge can be met–if we implement a large portfolio of solutions, the most important of which are eliminating fossil-fuel subsidies and putting a stiff price on carbon.

None of this will come as a shock to climate experts: our results were consistent with numerous reports that have argued against the silver bullet approach and in favor of "silver buckshot." But several things surprised the students. One was that planting a trillion trees doesn't help much, because it takes too long for them to grow. Another was that nuclear power doesn't help either, for essentially the same reason: nuclear plants take too long to build and bring online. Globally, the average construction time is about 10 years, and you need to add many years on to that period for site selection, regulatory approval and licensing. Some notorious examples have taken much longer. The most recent nuclear power reactors built in the U.S., at Georgia Power's Vogtle plant, were started in 2013 and are still not finished. That's the problem with imagined "breakthrough" technologies, too. Breakthroughs can be sudden, but implementation is slow.

I left the class thinking about nuclear power. Many people think nuclear energy is going to be the climate solution (or at least a big part of it). President Barack Obama included federal loan guarantees for nuclear power in his energy plan, in the hopes of jump-starting construction and garnering Republican support. (It did neither, but some Republicans are now pushing nuclear power as the key to cleaner U.S. energy.) If I want to rile up my Twitter feed, all I need do is post something even faintly skeptical about nuclear power, and its advocates come out in force, accusing me of being a Luddite, or a troglodyte, or worse.

What is it about nuclear energy that makes its advocates so determined in the face of what should be discouraging facts? After all, unlike futuristic, untried technologies, we have plenty of facts about this one, and most of them are discouraging.

The first American civilian nuclear power plant broke ground in Pennsylvania in 1954, around the same time that physicist John von Neumann predicted that, within a few decades, nuclear power would be so efficient as to make energy "free –just like the unmetered air– with coal and oil used mainly as raw materials for organic chemical synthesis." That didn't happen. Today nuclear power remains the most expensive form of electricity generation in the U.S.–typically costing twice as much to operate as a fossil-fuel-based plant. While the price of renewables has dropped dramatically, the cost of nuclear has remained stubbornly high. Nuclear fission is a technology with a track record of overpromising and underdelivering.

Why then do so many people keep coming back to it? I've come to think it's the same reason people turn to geoengineering and nuclear fusion (which has been "just around the corner" since 1943): the promise of technological progress. For the past century or more, humans have been accustomed to technological breakthroughs that made life easier, more comfortable and more entertaining. But climate change throws future advancement into doubt. It breaks the promise of progress. No matter what we do, we are going to be paying for the costs of our historical and current use of fossil fuels for decades to come.

So we turn to technofideism—the faith that technology will save us. Perhaps it will. But perhaps it won't, and our long-standing patterns of behavior will have to change along with our technology. And that's a hard pill to swallow.

About the Author

Naomi Oreskes is a professor of the history of science at Harvard University. She is author of Why Trust Science? *(Princeton University Press, 2019) and co-author of* Discerning Experts *(University of Chicago, 2019).*

Will Probiotics Save Corals or Harm Them?

By Elizabeth Svoboda

Manta rays and whitetip reef sharks glide past socially distanced visitors at Rio de Janeiro's hangar-sized AquaRio aquarium. In a laboratory upstairs, above the main gallery, a new experiment is underway, one that marine scientists hope will enhance the survival prospects of the world's coral reefs.

Twenty rectangular aquarium tanks, each about 20 centimeters wide, are arranged in a grid on the fourth floor. Each one houses a colorful assortment of coral fragments. The researchers will treat some tanks with cocktails of probiotics, a mix of bacteria designed to promote resilience under tough conditions.

Researcher João Rosado draws murky liquid into a pipette, then stands over the first tank and carefully depresses the plunger, squirting the mixture into the seawater. "Can you see that, like smoke?" says Rosado's colleague Pedro Cardoso of the Federal University of Rio de Janeiro, through his face mask. "Those are the bacteria." Cardoso is talking to me over a live video feed the team set up so I could witness the proceedings remotely. The gray bacterial cloud surrounds the coral like a shroud, settling on it. Later, Rosado will treat other tanks with probiotic-filled rotifers–microscopic marine animals that corals eat with their tiny mouths. Corals in a third set of tanks will get both treatments, and those in a fourth set will get none. The investigators will probe the various corals over the coming weeks to see if any of the regimens improve coral health.

The use of rotifers is a new attempt to get "good bacteria" to corals in distress. The results from the December 2020 experiment will help inform biologists' intention to apply probiotics to reefs in the wild in hopes of improving their chances of surviving the high temperatures and disease outbreaks that are overwhelming them.

Rosado and Cardoso's trial–led by marine biologist Gustavo Duarte–builds on work by their mentor, Raquel Peixoto, who published the first probiotics experiments in 2015. She is a leader of the audacious and controversial rescue plan to administer probiotics in the ocean, which could change the ecosystem. Peixoto will apply probiotics in the Red Sea later this year, and conservation groups are eagerly exploring the concept. Although Peixoto and her contemporaries have conducted many lab experiments and will carefully restrict the first open-ocean tests, she says corals are so threatened it is "time for us to take some risks."

Coral reefs cover nearly 285,000 square kilometers of ocean floor worldwide. They are largely concentrated into a dozen major chains, but they exert a global influence on marine and human life. Almost a quarter of marine species spend at least some part of their lives there. The reefs dampen storm surges and waves that can tear apart shorelines. They feed millions of people and account for almost $20 billion annually in global tourism.

Yet the world's corals are in a state of possibly terminal decline. Scientists first observed mass coral bleaching–a sign of starvation–in 1983, and by the 1990s they had started to link bleaching to changing sea temperatures. Between 1987 and 2019, oceans warmed 450 percent more than they did between 1955 and 1986. Since 1980, 94 percent of coral reefs have experienced at least one episode of severe bleaching. The Great Barrier Reef has suffered three such events in the past five years. A report from the United Nations Environment Program estimates that largely because of ocean warming, most of the planet's reefs will suffer annual severe bleaching by 2034 and, without intervention, will be gone entirely by 2100. Global reef death most likely will continue even if countries begin to get their carbon emissions under control. To reverse the trend, "we have a very narrow window of time–basically a decade," says Carlos M. Duarte, a marine ecologist at King Abdullah University of Science and Technology (KAUST) in Saudi Arabia. "The window is rapidly closing."

Scientists developing probiotics see the treatments as more than a stopgap to postpone reef death. They think probiotics have a real chance to reverse some damage that has already been done, enabling once threatened corals to flourish and strengthening new human-bred corals that are transplanted onto ailing reefs. "It sounds so radical," says Rebecca Vega Thurber, a marine microbial ecologist at Oregon State University. But, she adds, "with proper experimental design and application, it could be helpful."

Big questions still need answers. When applied at sea, will probiotics wash away? Would the labor-intensive techniques cost huge sums of money when tried across reefs hundreds of kilometers long? And even the most avid backers acknowledge the risk they are running. In some ways, reef treatments sound a bit like geoengineering–sprinkling iron into the sea to encourage growth of algae that soak up carbon dioxide or spraying aerosols into the air to reflect the sun's rays back to space, lessening global warming. Seeding reefs with bacteria might alter the ocean ecosystem at a fundamental level.

Some experts worry that certain bacteria could accidentally spawn new coral disease outbreaks, a possibility that arose in a recent lab test. And no one knows exactly how the treatments will affect ocean life further up the food chain, such as fish and crabs that feed on coral polyps.

As with climate change, however, the global prospects for reefs have become so dire that many conservationists think extreme fixes are needed. "It's not a good position for scientists to be [in]," says Peixoto, now a marine microbiologist at KAUST. But she says the decision is clear. "We have to act. Otherwise, it's going to be too late."

Reef Repair

Researchers have been trying to restore damaged reefs since the 1970s. In 2000 Baruch Rinkevich of Israel's National Institute of Oceanography started one of the first nurseries to raise young corals and transplant them onto reefs that had suffered damage from fishing, diving or storms.

Scientists started looking into specific fixes for bleaching a few years after that. In 2010 researchers at Florida's Mote Marine Laboratory showed that by chipping fragments off of healthy corals in lab tanks they could trigger a Herculean growth response that promptly turns those fragments into full-fledged baby corals. (Corals can reproduce sexually by releasing eggs and sperm into the ocean or asexually by budding–essentially, cloning.) In 2018 and 2019 researchers in Mexico and Israel used the Mote team's strategy to generate coral fragments and transplant them onto reefs just off Mexico's Pacific coast. The new corals that grew from them showed an impressive survival rate of about 60 percent, despite the damaging effects of Hurricane Willa. On Florida's reefs, corals the Mote team has grown from fragments merged into larger colonies that in 2020 began successfully spawning in the wild.

Breeding is another strategy. Since at least 2015 researchers at the Australian Institute of Marine Science (AIMS) and elsewhere have been trying in labs to selectively breed so-called super corals, which carry genes that help the animals withstand stress. Teams at the institute and the University of Hawaii's Gates Coral Lab are creating these ultraresilient corals using "assisted evolution," which involves selecting wild corals with desirable genetic traits, such as the ability to survive high ocean temperatures, then cross-breeding them to yield offspring with an abundance of the traits. In a 2020 lab study at AIMS, temperature-tolerant corals created this way proved up to 26 times more likely to survive extreme heat than other corals.

Yet another approach to helping corals is to enhance reproduction. In 2017 a team at the California Academy of Sciences, the Nature Conservancy and SECORE International, a conservation organization, began catching the eggs and sperm that healthy spawning corals release in the wild on rare but predictable nights. The researchers complete the fertilization in the lab, then transplant larvae onto needy reefs.

These techniques share a daunting drawback: restoration workers have to manipulate corals in a lab and refine ways to transplant them onto struggling reefs, a slow and costly process. It could be quicker and more affordable if a therapeutic could be administered directly to ailing corals in the wild. That prospect helped to lead researchers such as Peixoto to probiotics. And, theoretically at least, selectively bred lab corals, or chipped fragments, could also be treated with probiotics to make them more resistant to heat and disease before they are transplanted in the sea.

Coral formations are constellations of thousands of animals called polyps, each often smaller than a pinky fingernail. Every polyp hosts a variety of bacteria, algae, fungi and other microorganisms, collectively known as its microbiome. Like microbes in the human gut, these tiny residents carry out tasks that keep the whole system functioning. In recent years metagenomic analysis–sequencing the genes of the microbes on a polyp–has supplied a clearer picture of which tasks the microbes are performing. Scientists at the Massachusetts Institute of Technology, the Woods Hole Oceanographic Institute, and elsewhere have isolated bacteria that consume excess nitrogen, preventing nearby algal blooms that starve coral of nutrients. Other microorganisms degrade reactive oxygen species–molecules that damage coral cells–or help corals capture carbon for energy. Much as microbes in the human gut help to break down food, contributing to our nutrition and health, researchers theorize that beneficial coral microbes make the hosts more resilient to environmental stresses by supporting their overall health and warding off polyp disease and tissue loss.

As ocean temperatures rise, however, the microbial relationships within corals start to break down. Scientists at Oregon State University have found that bacterial communities on stressed corals often become unstable, potentially giving disease-causing microbes a chance to spread. Warming oceans, together with ocean acidification caused by higher carbon dioxide levels, also disrupt the microbe-aided calcification process that gives corals their structure, making it harder for them to repair damage. At the same time, stressed polyps expel their *Symbiodinium* algae, which turn sunlight into food for polyps, leaving them without a food source. This gives corals a characteristic bleached appearance that biologists recognize as a sign of doom because bleached polyps are also more vulnerable to disease. Peixoto has witnessed this alarming transformation firsthand.

A Disintegrating Universe

As a kid on vacation, Peixoto snorkeled the Brazilian reefs near Bahia, entranced by the vivid universe beneath her. On dives as an adult, she saw that universe disintegrating. Corals were turning into lifeless skeletons; the ones that were hanging on looked wan and sickly. "Every year is getting worse," she says. "You dive and see 90 percent of the species dead." Peixoto resolved to do something transformative, something that could revive wild corals. "We want to protect the diversity already there in the reef," she says, "to make sure colonies can survive."

She had a novel starting point in mind. In a 2010 experiment aimed at developing an alternative to the hazardous chemicals used to clean up oil spills in Brazilian mangroves, her team demonstrated that oil-sucking bacteria could break down the oil and promote plant health and growth. What if she could summon concentrated bacterial reinforcements to protect coral reefs? No one had tried probiotics, but she had a hunch they might work.

As a first move, Peixoto harvested tissue and seawater from the surfaces of local corals. Then she sequenced the bacterial genes in that mix to find species that carry out functions promoting survival. She grew the native microbes in culture and mixed bespoke cocktails for each reef environment. Her work paid off in late 2018, when she and her colleagues published a study showing that their tailored probiotic blend helped corals survive hot aquarium temperatures and resist disease.

One of Peixoto's newest experiments, being reviewed by journals, goes deeper, appearing to show distinct mechanisms that probiotics may use to enhance corals' health. Her team in Brazil placed four finger-length coral segments in each of 20 small tanks and assembled a cocktail of six bacterial strains from healthy *Mussismilia hispida*, a common South Atlantic coral. Every few days they removed a few segments, dripped a dot of probiotics onto their surfaces, and returned them to the tanks. Next they raised the water temperature on half the tanks.

The results weeks later were dramatic: more than a third of the control corals had died, but almost all the treated corals were alive. Detailed analysis revealed multiple ways the probiotics appeared to promote health. The treated corals less strongly expressed genes linked to inflammation. They also showed less gene activity related to cell death. That means corals "can even bleach, but it's not to the extent that they lose tissue," Peixoto says. "The probiotics provide them with this kind of buffer." That buffer could give other restoration measures–such as super-coral breeding or spawning baby corals from fragments–a better chance to work. The right probiotics applied in the lab before transplantation could potentially increase the corals' odds of survival.

The First Field Trial

On a crisp day in January 2020, scientists at Florida's Smithsonian Marine Station applied a probiotic to coral in the ocean, the first time that had been tried. The probiotic, which they had been developing for three years, wasn't a broad-spectrum blend like Peixoto's. It was designed to counter a specific threat, one of the gravest to Florida's reefs: stony coral tissue-loss disease. Researcher Kelly Pitts, who had joined the team in 2019 after working on antibiotic treatments at Nova Southeastern University, wanted to test probiotics as a more natural aid for coral health. She donned her oxygen tank and fins and descended from a small boat onto a reef ringing Florida's eastern coastline off of Fort Lauderdale. At roughly nine meters deep, as Pitts tells the story, a clear plastic bag about half a meter across and pinned to the seafloor came into view, enclosing a coral formation like a dome.

The target inside was a great star coral that was more than a decade old (colonies can thrive for decades or even centuries). Some of the polyps were still a vibrant orange, but others had faded to khaki, a sign they might have been ravaged by stony coral tissue-loss disease. Pitts snaked a flexible tube under the dome's edge, then attached a bacteria-filled syringe to her end of the tube. As she lowered the plunger, murky white liquid bloomed in the dome, thick enough to obscure the coral.

Pitts was excited but anxious. Her team had been testing its probiotics in tanks for months, but being out on the reef was completely different. What if the mixture escaped the bag? She felt the same apprehension during another test months later when she squeezed a probiotic gel, like toothpaste from a tube, onto a coral on the seafloor that was fully exposed to the water, no bag to encapsulate it. When the paste stuck fast to the coral despite surrounding water currents, her nervousness gave way to elation, and she laughed with joy, clapping her hands underwater.

Stony coral tissue-loss disease, which eats through polyps like acid, had laid waste to more than 96,000 acres of reef in Florida and the Caribbean since 2014. The disease—suspected to be bacterial—was spreading unchecked, killing large formations within weeks or months. By 2017 quelling the outbreak had zoomed to the top of the priority list for Florida conservationists. Using rapid gene sequencing, the Smithsonian Marine Station researchers identified a *Pseudoalteromonas* bacterium, present in small quantities on local corals, that produced the marine antibiotic korormicin.* In aquarium tests, concentrated doses of the probiotic bacteria kept the disease at bay.

During lab tests the researchers applied the bacteria to a range of corals from the broader reef to be sure it would not harm any healthy species. In a rush to get the disease under control, Florida researchers had been dosing corals with antibiotics such as amoxicillin since 2018—a drastic measure that was also killing scads of beneficial bacteria. Pitts hoped probiotics could get around that indiscriminate injury.

In late 2019 the Smithsonian team secured the state permits needed to plunge into ocean trials. Researchers were cautious and were mindful of the need to start small, but the disease was spreading so fast local conservationists were in favor of the proposed test run.

During the January 2020 field trial and another in September 2020, Pitts and her colleagues treated 14 coral formations using the dome method and seven others with the paste. When the team did an initial survey of the reef two weeks after the January trial, the disease's progress had stopped in about 80 percent of the treated corals. Some of their patchy lesions were also beginning to heal. The growing COVID-19 pandemic, however, caused scientists to pause trials for a time.

Unintended Consequences

All microbiology is contextual. Changing the concentrations of one "beneficial" type of coral bacteria can affect other key bacteria in the microbiome in ways that are hard to predict. For skeptics of coral probiotics, this complexity and unpredictability is a source of unease. "Maybe the function is temporarily good," Vega Thurber says. "But it could easily switch to be something that has a negative effect."

Hawaii Institute of Marine Biology molecular ecologist Ty Roach, who has done his own probiotic lab tests, worries about irreversibly changing a coral microbiome or an entire marine ecosystem. "The more I've tinkered with it, the more I'm concerned," he says. In one unpublished study of his involving about 130 finger-length *Porites* corals in a dozen three-gallon tanks, some of the corals died of disease after his team inoculated them with a dose of their own native bacteria (not a tailored cocktail like those Peixoto makes). The first trouble Roach noticed was that certain corals formed thick sheets of mucus on their surfaces, as if they were irritated. Then small patches of polyp tissue started to die, like spreading canker sores. Roach was alarmed but not surprised. The coral's natural bacterial mix includes microbes from the *Staphylococcus* genus, which is known to cause disease in humans.

Roach adds that there is scant peer-reviewed research that describes the exact biological mechanisms by which probiotics might protect coral hosts. "We've been able to make some corals withstand a little more heat," Roach says. "How that works is very unclear." And he wonders whether the treatments will affect other marine life. "A lot of other organisms are in direct interaction with these corals on the reef," he says, including fish, algae and crustaceans. University of Derby aquatic biologist Michael Sweet, a longtime colleague and friend of Peixoto's, supports probiotic methods if they can be proven safe. But he also echoes Roach's concerns: "I don't want to be the one responsible for releasing a superbug into the environment that becomes the next coral disease."

How often probiotic treatments should be applied is also unknown. Human probiotics for digestive disorders often need to be taken every day or even twice a day. Researchers can only guess if applications, say, once a week or once a month would be enough to create a resilient microbial equilibrium.

Risk is just one practical consideration. At this stage, the cost of applying cocktails across an entire reef is hard to calculate. Peixoto says a little of the mixes she has created goes a long way, but it might cost up to $600 to $700 to treat one square kilometer of reef, assuming trained divers apply the probiotics (and assuming they have a dive boat of their own). An application might protect corals from heat damage for up to a month. On a wide scale, robots built for applying the compounds would be less expensive than human divers, she says.

Sweet recently reported that creating lab-grown corals through assisted evolution–transplanting them on a reef and monitoring them–would cost between $49 and $227 for each coral colony. Reefs often have tens of thousands of colonies per square kilometer. If probiotic bacteria were added to the lab-grown corals before transplant, the added cost "would be low," Sweet says. But "if we need to redeploy the probiotics regularly, it could become an expensive method."

Yet Roach and Sweet also know that reefs are in such peril that conservation funders will likely forge ahead with probiotics in the wild. "If there's one thing we've learned," says marine biologist Crawford Drury, Roach's Hawaii colleague, it is that "if we start losing reefs, the willingness to do something extreme skyrockets."

Indeed, big organizations are embracing the idea. The World Wildlife Fund in Brazil, which is financing some of Peixoto's research, is optimistic about the technique's prospects. In Brazil, the massive reef bleaching event of 2019 "turned the key" to exploring newer conservation options such as probiotics, says Vinicius Nora, a WWF Brazil conservation analyst. Australia's Great Barrier Reef Foundation, which has committed hundreds of thousands of dollars to probiotics research, also sees Peixoto's treatments as a promising way to fortify lab-grown coral intended for transplant. Foundation officials are working with Peixoto and Australian scientists to include probiotics in future restoration projects if further small-scale tests go well. "It's a catch-up that we're having to do," foundation biologist Ove Hoegh-Guldberg says. "You've got to jump in with boots on and test a few ideas."

Radical Determination

Peixoto understands her critics' concerns. To help ease some minds, including her own, she is planning contained experiments this year at the 700-square-meter artificial ocean in the University of Arizona's Biosphere 2. The tests will give a clearer look at how probiotic treatments might affect other ocean life. Still, she doesn't spend a lot of time second-guessing her course. She admits she gets impatient with people who call for too much caution. She feels a moral obligation to use all means to save reefs. For Peixoto, that means deploying coral probiotics in oceans very soon. "If we don't do anything," she says, "they will die."

Her next act will be staged at KAUST, which sits on a spit of Saudi Arabian coast that curls into the Red Sea like a lobster claw. From the docks, Peixoto can step into her dive boat and motor out to a shallow reef 10 minutes away, where schools of golden butterflyfish cruise over decades-old coral monoliths on the seafloor.

Because Red Sea reefs have thrived for years in high-temperature water, bacteria that limit heat damage here could help scientists learn how to confer heat resistance onto ailing corals elsewhere. The reef, Peixoto says, "is like my vault. I go there and get the gold." Yet even stalwart Red Sea corals are starting to show signs of stress. A bleaching event devastated sections of reef in 2020, and experts fear worse is to come. Peixoto is fine-tuning a blend of bacteria she hopes to apply on the reef this year, while still ramping up experiments in Biosphere 2. The trial will be the first time she and her team test probiotics in the ocean.

Some Red Sea reef formations are separated by long stretches of empty seafloor. This will make it easier for Peixoto to apply probiotics to one formation while leaving the next-closest ones untouched. "These will be very small and well-controlled experiments," she says.

Even so, the test will be a different approach than what the Smithsonian team used in Florida. The Smithsonian's treatment was a single microbe deployed to treat a specific coral disease. Peixoto will dose corals with a multistrain cocktail that has a much broader aim—to fortify corals against bleaching and the ill health that follows. As in the past, Peixoto will isolate beneficial microbes from local corals and mix them into a custom slurry. She will exclude any groups of bacteria known to cause disease and will first conduct detailed risk assessments in tanks at the university to make sure the cocktail does not cause any adverse coral health effects in a small setting.

If that test goes smoothly, she will eventually apply her mix to several reef formations, about two square meters each. The microbes will be delivered via strips of time-release, water-resistant adhesive that sticks to the corals or to nearby sediment. After a few weeks Peixoto will assess how the health of treated corals compares with that of controls. Periodic checks will continue for a year, and throughout the process she will monitor nearby fish and other large organisms such as sponges for unintended bacterial effects.

Peixoto recognizes the magnitude of this next act, but the widening coral ghost towns she sees on her dives have strengthened her commitment to err on the side of radical intervention. She is an optimist, with an innovator's faith in the power of bioremediation. She knows some people might call her hasty. Yet Peixoto and others think bold intervention is simply required now. "If we develop all the technologies, we can still have beautiful reefs," she says, "rehabilitated reefs that can thrive." Without that targeted assistance, she sees a long undersea dark ages ahead.

*Editor's Note (4/27/21): This sentence was revised after posting to correct the name of the bacterium that was identified.

About the Author

Elizabeth Svoboda is a science writer in San Jose, Calif., and author of What Makes a Hero?: The Surprising Science of Selflessness *(Penguin Group, 2013).*

Utility-Scale Energy Storage Will Enable a Renewable Grid

By Andrea Thompson

The way the world gets its electricity is undergoing a rapid transition, driven by both the increased urgency of decarbonizing energy systems and the plummeting costs of wind and solar technology. In the past decade electricity generated by renewables in the U.S. has doubled, primarily from wind and solar installations, according to the Energy Information Administration. In January 2019 the EIA forecast that wind, solar and other nonhydroelectric renewables would be the fastest-growing slice of the electricity portfolio for the next two years. But the intermittent nature of those sources means that electric utilities need a way to keep energy in their back pocket for when the sun is not shining and the winds are calm. That need is increasing interest in energy-storage technology–in particular, lithium-ion batteries, which are finally poised to be more than just a bit player in the grid.

For decades pumped-storage hydropower, a simple process that features reservoirs at different elevations, has been the dominant large-scale energy-storage method in the U.S. To store energy, water is pumped into the higher reservoir; when that energy is needed, the water is released into the lower reservoir, flowing through a turbine along the way. Pumped-storage hydropower currently accounts for 95 percent of U.S. utility-scale energy storage, according to the Department of Energy. But as efficiency and reliability have improved, and manufacturing costs have tumbled, lithium-ion batteries have surged. They account for more than 80 percent of the U.S.'s utility-scale battery-storage power capacity, which jumped from just a few megawatts a decade ago to 866 megawatts by February 2019, the EIA says. A March 2019 analysis by Bloomberg New Energy Finance reports that the cost of electricity from such batteries has dropped by 76 percent since 2012, making them close to competitive with the plants, typically powered by natural gas, that are switched on during times of high electricity demand. To date, whereas batteries have largely been used to make brief, quick adjustments to maintain power levels, utilities in several states, including Florida and California, are adding lithium-ion batteries that will be able to last for two to four hours. Energy research firm Wood Mackenzie estimates that the market for energy storage will double from 2018 to 2019 and triple from 2019 to 2020.

Lithium-ion batteries will likely be the dominant technology for the next five to 10 years, according to experts, and continuing improvements will result in batteries that can store four to eight hours of energy–long enough, for example, to shift solar-generated power to the evening peak in demand.

But getting to the point where renewables and energy storage can handle the baseline load of electricity generation will take energy storage at longer timescales, which will mean moving beyond lithium-ion batteries. Potential candidates range from other high-tech options, such as flow batteries, which pump liquid electrolytes, and hydrogen fuel cells to simpler concepts, such as pumped-storage hydropower and what is called gravity storage. Pumped-storage hydropower is cheap once it is installed, but it is expensive to build and can be used only in certain terrain. Similarly simple is the concept of gravity storage, which purports to use spare electricity to raise a heavy block that can later be lowered to drive a turbine to generate electricity. Although a few companies are working on demonstrations and have attracted investments, the idea has yet to take off. Other options are still under development to make them sufficiently reliable, efficient and cost-competitive with lithium-ion batteries. There were only three large-scale flow-battery storage systems deployed in the U.S. by the end of 2017, according to the EIA, and utility-scale hydrogen systems remain in demonstration stages. The U.S. government is funding some work in this arena, particularly through the Advanced Research Projects Agency–Energy (ARPA-E), but much of the investment in those technologies–and in energy storage in general–is happening in China and South Korea, which have also ramped up storage research.

It is uncertain whether and how much the costs of energy storage will continue to decline. Yet the accumulating pledges by governments–including at the state and local level in the U.S.–to achieve carbon-free electricity production will provide a continued push to bring more and more storage online.

About the Author

Andrea Thompson, an associate editor at Scientific American, covers sustainability. Follow her on Twitter @AndreaTWeather

GLOSSARY

albedo Measure of the amount of light a surface reflects.

bomb cyclone Storm pattern characterized by a rapid drop in air pressure and excessive precipitation.

climate refugee Someone who has been forced to flee their home due to climate change and its broader social impacts.

consensus Point of agreement among a group of people.

El Niño–Southern Oscillation A recurring alternation of surface water temperatures in the Pacific Ocean, which impacts rainfall and temperature patterns around the world.

feedback When the results of a process influence the beginning of a process; in climate, feedback either slows down or speeds up warming.

granular Characterized by a high level of focus or detail.

infrastructure The built facilities and staff that support basic social activities.

jet stream Air currents in the Earth's Northern and Southern Hemispheres that play a significant role in regulating global weather patterns.

La Niña A weather pattern that often follows El Niño. It involves cold surface water upwelling along South America's western coast and influences weather in other parts of the world.

mitigation Efforts to reduce or counteract the harms caused by something.

resplendent Visually pleasing, with bright colors or rich details.

sequestration Capturing and storing carbon dioxide in an attempt to reduce atmospheric carbon levels.

solidarity Mutual support and care among members of a community or group.

FURTHER INFORMATION

Daley, Jim. "Deforestation Intensifies Warming in the Amazon Rain Forest." *Scientific American*, September 18, 2019, https://www.scientificamerican.com/article/deforestation-intensifies-warming-in-the-amazon-rain-forest1/.

Fialka, John. "Should We Change Earth to Halt Warming?" *Scientific American*, July 11, 2017, https://www.scientificamerican.com/article/should-we-change-earth-to-halt-warming/.

Fischetti, Mark, and Katie Peek. "A New Reality Up North." *Scientific American*, August 1, 2019, https://www.scientificamerican.com/article/a-new-reality-up-north1/.

Harrington, Samantha. "How Extreme Weather Threatens People with Disabilities." *Scientific American*, September 18, 2019, https://www.scientificamerican.com/article/how-extreme-weather-threatens-people-with-disabilities/.

Harvey, Chelsea. "More and More Links Are Emerging between Warming and Extreme Weather." *Scientific American*, December 10, 2019, https://www.scientificamerican.com/article/more-and-more-links-are-emerging-between-warming-and-extreme-weather/.

Intergovernmental Panel on Climate Change. *Climate Change 2022: Impacts, Adaptation, and Vulnerability*. Working Group II Contribution to the IPCC Sixth Assessment Report. 2022, https://www.ipcc.ch/report/ar6/wg2/.

Rich, Nathaniel. "Losing Earth: The Decade We Almost Stopped Climate Change." *The New York Times Magazine*, August 1, 2018, https://www.nytimes.com/interactive/2018/08/01/magazine/climate-change-losing-earth.html.

Sabin Center for Climate Change Law. *Climate Attribution Database*. Columbia University, 2022, https://climateattribution.org/.

CITATIONS

1.1 The Arctic Is Breaking Climate Records, Altering Weather Worldwide by Jennifer A. Francis (April 1, 2018); 1.2 What Ancient Mass Extinctions Tell Us about the Future by Peter Brannen (September 1, 2020); 1.3 The Hidden Figure in Climate Science by Dawn Starin (August 26, 2019); 1.4 Global Warming: How Hot, Exactly, Is It Going to Get? by Kate Marvel (May 12, 2019); 1.5 Why We Know about the Greenhouse Gas Effect by David Wogan (May 16, 2013); 2.1 Marine Oxygen Levels Are the Next Great Casualty of Climate Change by Nathalie Goodkin, Julie Pullen (November 23, 2021); 2.2 Scientists Are Taking Extreme Steps to Help Corals Survive by Rebecca Albright (January 1, 2018); 2.3 Australia's Angry Summer: This Is What Climate Change Looks Like by Nerilie Abram (December 31, 2019); 2.4 Yes, Climate Change Is Making Severe Weather Worse by Jennifer Francis (June 1, 2019); 3.1 The Unfolding Tragedy of Climate Change in Bangladesh by Robert Glennon (April 21, 2017); 3.2 How Climate Change Is Making It Harder to Predict Outbreaks by Lois Parshley (May 1, 2018); 3.3 Climate Change Hastened Syria's Civil War by Mark Fischetti (March 2, 2015); 3.4 Climate Change Is Creating New Vocabulary, from Eco-Anxiety to Kaitiakitanga by Trish Stewart (November 5, 2021); 3.5 How Cities Can Protect Themselves from Rising Waters by Ziqian (Cecilia) Dong (March 28, 2019); 4.1 Three Things We Must Do to Tackle Climate Change by Susan Joy Hassol, Jerry Melillo (November 2, 2021); 4.2 Climate Deniers Shift Tactics to 'Inactivism' by Richard Schiffman (January 12, 2021); 4.3 To Understand How Science Denial Works, Look to History by Naomi Oreskes (December 1, 2020); 4.4 Our Environmental Crisis Requires Political Fixes, Not Technological Ones by Peter Sutoris (February 7, 2022); 4.5 These Alternative Economies Are Inspirations for a Sustainable World by Ashish Kothari (June 1, 2021); 4.6 Fossil-Fuel Subsidies Must End by Geoffrey Supran, Peter Erickson, Doug Koplow, Michael Lazarus, Peter Newell, Naomi Oreskes, Harro van Asselt (February 24, 2020); 5.1 The Economist Takes a Strange Turn on Science by Tali Trigg (February 26, 2016); 5.2 The Best Technology for Fighting Climate Change Isn't a Technology by Han de Groot (December 5, 2018); 5.3 Can Natural Gas Be Part of a Low-Carbon Future? by Michael E. Webber (April 1, 2021); 5.4 New Nuclear Power Plants Are Unlikely to Stop the Climate Crisis by Naomi Oreskes (February 1, 2022); 5.5 Will Probiotics Save Corals or Harm Them? by Elizabeth Svoboda (May 1, 2021); 5.6 Utility-Scale Energy Storage Will Enable a Renewable Grid by Andrea Thompson (July 1, 2019).

Each author biography was accurate at the time the article was originally published.

INDEX